THE ARAB-ISRAELI CONFLICT

Alex Woolf

WORLD ALMANAC® LIBRARY

Please visit our web site at: www.worldalmanaclibrary.com
For a free color catalog describing World Almanac® Library's list of high-quality books
and multimedia programs, call 1-800-848-2928 (USA) or 1-800-387-3178 (Canada).
World Almanac® Library's fax: (414) 332-3567.

Library of Congress Cataloging-in-Publication Data

Woolf, Alex, 1964-
    The Arab-Israeli conflict / by Alex Woolf.
       p. cm. — (Atlas of conflicts)
    Includes bibliographical references and index.
    ISBN 0-8368-5665-1 (lib. bdg.)
    ISBN 0-8368-5672-4 (softcover)
    1. Arab-Israeli conflict—Juvenile literature. I. Title. II. Series.
  DS119.7.W63   2004
  956.04—dc22   2004045157

This North American edition first published in 2005 by
World Almanac® Library
330 West Olive Street, Suite 100
Milwaukee, WI 53212 USA

Produced by Arcturus Publishing Limited.
Series concept: Alex Woolf
Editor: Philip de Ste. Croix
Designer: Simon Burrough
Cartography: The Map Studio
Consultant: Paul Cornish, Imperial War Museum, London
Picture researcher: Thomas Mitchell

World Almanac® Library editor: Jim Mezzanotte
World Almanac® Library design: Steve Schraenkler
World Almanac® Library production: Jessica Morris

All the photographs in this book, with the exception of those listed below, were supplied by
Getty Images and are reproduced here with their permission.
Camera Press: page 33 (David Rubinger).
Topham/AP: pages 36, 43, 44.

Printed in Italy

1 2 3 4 5 6 7 8 9 08 07 06 05 04

CONTENTS

CHAPTER 1
THE FOUNDING OF ISRAEL

Jewish immigrants arriving in New York City circa 1920. During the early decades of the twentieth century, many thousands of Jews fled persecution in Europe to seek a new life in the United States.

The conflict between Palestinian Arabs and Jews began in the late nineteenth century and intensified after the establishment of the Jewish nation of Israel in 1948. The conflict is essentially about land and who controls it. The land in question is a small region on the eastern coast of the Mediterranean Sea with an area of about 10,036 square miles (26,000 square kilometers). It was the historical site of the Jewish kingdoms of Israel and Judah during the first millennium B.C., and even today most Jews feel that they have a historic, traditional, or religious connection to the land. The Palestinian Arabs' claim to the region is based on the fact that they have lived there continuously for hundreds of years.

During the nineteenth century, there was a rise in anti-Semitism (hostility toward Jews) in many parts of eastern Europe and Russia. This anti-Semitism was rooted in religious antagonisms and the perceived wealth and economic power of the Jews. Beginning in the 1880s, many Jewish communities came under severe attack. By 1914, some five million Jews had fled to new homes in the United States, Britain, Canada, Australia, and South Africa.

Some Jews believed that Jewish people would never be safe from anti-Semitism if they remained minorities in the countries where they lived, and that Jews needed a homeland of their own. To that end, in the 1890s a movement called Zionism emerged. Zion was one of the hills of Jerusalem, the capital of the historical land of Israel. The Zionists sought to establish a Jewish nation on the site of ancient Israel.

At that time, the land they wished to reclaim was known as Palestine and was governed by the Turkish Ottoman Empire, which extended throughout the Middle East. In the 1880s, about 462,000 people lived in Palestine, including 447,000 Arabs and 15,000 Jews. The Zionist movement led to a large rise in Jewish immigration to Palestine. By 1914, about 60,000 Jews, or 10 per cent of the population, lived in Palestine. The Palestinian Arabs were unhappy about these new Jewish settlers and at times clashed with them.

In the late nineteenth century, Arabs throughout the Middle East began to develop an awareness of themselves as a separate nation, and there was a

The bodies of Jewish men killed in a campaign of anti-Semitic persecution in Ukraine circa 1900.

HOMELAND

"Palestine is our unforgettable historic homeland. . . . The Jews who will it shall achieve their State. We shall live at last as free men on our own soil, and in our own homes peacefully die. The world will be liberated by our freedom, enriched by our wealth, magnified by our greatness. And whatever we attempt there for our own benefit will redound mightily and beneficially to the good of all mankind."

—From *Der Judenstaat,*
Theodor Herzl

Below: Russian Jews work on a kibbutz (commune) in Palestine in 1912. Between 1880 and 1914, over 60,000 former Russian or eastern European Jews settled on land in Palestine or worked as hired laborers.

Above: Palestine under Ottoman rule was divided into sanjaks, or sub-provinces. (A wilayat is a province.) Between 1900 and 1918, Zionist colonies rose in number from 19 to 47. The Palestinians lobbied their Turkish leaders to end Jewish immigration and land purchases by Zionists.

growing movement to overthrow their Turkish rulers. The Ottoman Empire was in decline, and the great powers of Europe—Britain, France, and Germany—were looking for ways to extend their influence in the area.

The British government made secret contact with Arab nationalist leaders in 1915 to 1916 and persuaded them to rise against the Ottoman Empire, which was then an ally of Germany. In return, Britain promised to support the establishment of an independent Arab state in the Arab territories of the Ottoman Empire, including Palestine.

In 1917, however, Britain also announced its support for the establishment of a Jewish homeland. Called the Balfour Declaration, for British foreign minister Arthur Balfour, this support contradicted Britain's earlier promise to the Arabs.

After the fall of the Ottoman Empire in 1921, the status of the empire's former territories was discussed at a meeting of the League of Nations, an organization of countries established in 1919 to promote international peace and security. In an agreement known as the British Mandate, Palestine was placed under British control. Arabs were angry that Britain did not fulfill its promise to create an independent Arab state, and they were also worried by the increasing numbers of Jews arriving from Europe. Clashes between the Arabs and Zionist Jews grew increasingly violent during the 1920s and 1930s. Jewish immigration to Palestine continued to rise, however, particularly after the anti-Semitic Nazi Party came to power in Germany in 1933.

THE UNITED NATIONS PARTITION

After the Holocaust—the systematic extermination of nearly six million European Jews by the Nazis during World War II—Jewish demands for an independent homeland in Palestine grew much harder to ignore. The British authorities, faced with growing Arab-Jewish violence as well as terrorist attacks against government buildings by Zionist militias, sought to

THE BALFOUR DECLARATION

"His Majesty's Government view with favour the establishment in Palestine of a national home for the Jewish people, and will use their best endeavours to facilitate the achievement of this object, it being clearly understood that nothing shall be done which may prejudice the civil and religious rights of existing non-Jewish communities in Palestine, or the rights and political status enjoyed by Jews in any other country."

—From the Balfour Declaration, November 2, 1917

British army officer T.E. Lawrence, better known as Lawrence of Arabia, was a champion of Arab nationalism. He helped organize an Arab revolt against the Turks during World War I.

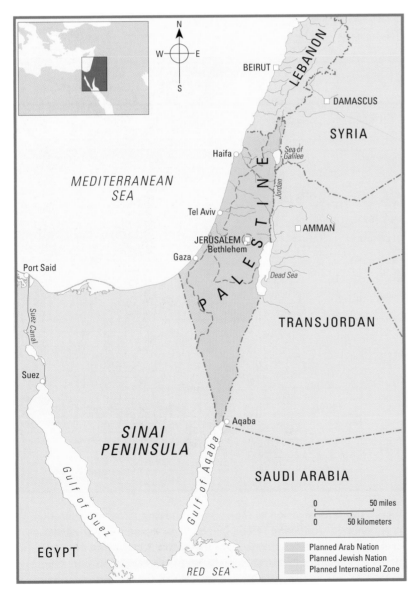

end their mandate. In 1947, they requested help from the United Nations (UN). A successor to the League of Nations, this organization of countries was formed in 1945 with the same goal of promoting international peace and security.

To resolve the Arab-Jewish conflict, a UN committee proposed dividing Palestine into two nations. The partition plan ensured that one nation would have a majority of Arabs and the other nation would have a majority of Jews. The Jewish nation would control 55 per cent of Palestine. Under the plan, the disputed area containing Jerusalem and Bethlehem would become an international zone.

THE 1947–1949 WAR Zionist leaders agreed to the plan, although they were unhappy not to be offered Jerusalem, a sacred city to the Jews. The Arabs rejected the plan. They believed the UN had acted under Zionist pressure to grant statehood to the Jewish settlers. On November 29, 1947, the UN General Assembly voted to accept the plan. Within days, military conflict erupted between Palestinian Arabs and Jews. The first phase of the fighting lasted until April 1, 1948. It took the form of a low-level guerrilla conflict between small Arab and Jewish forces, with many gunfights but no major battles. Little territory was gained by either side. The British administration's authority had declined to such an extent that they were powerless to keep order and simply let the two sides fight between themselves.

On April 1, 1948, Zionist forces took the initiative. Within weeks, they had captured most of the territory allotted to them under the UN plan. On May 15, 1948, the British departed from Palestine, and Zionist leaders declared the founding of the state of Israel. Neighboring Arab nations—Egypt, Syria, Lebanon, Saudi Arabia, Transjordan, and Iraq, which lay to the east of Transjordan—immediately invaded the new country. They did so, they stated, to save Palestine from the Zionists. They also had ambitions, however, to control parts of Palestine themselves.

Although the Israeli forces were fewer in number than their Arab opponents, they were better trained

Above: During the 1947–1949 war, Israeli soldiers prepare to launch an attack on Egyptian forces before capturing the Negev Desert in what is now southern Israel.

Above: The Arab invasion of May 1948, following Israel's declaration of nationhood. Jordanian forces launched an assault on Jerusalem as Iraqi troops took up positions in various West Bank towns. An Egyptian attack in the south, meanwhile, wiped out several Israeli kibbutzim, and Syrian and Lebanese forces penetrated parts of northern Israel.

and organized. The battle was evenly balanced during the first two months of fighting, but when secret arms shipments began reaching Israel from Europe, the war swung in Israel's favor, and its forces began capturing territories beyond those granted by the UN partition.

The war ended when the UN arranged a series of cease-fires between the Arabs and Jews in late 1948. Armistice agreements were signed by Israel and the Arab states between February and July 1949. Under these agreements, former Palestine was divided into three parts. Israel controlled over 77 per cent of the territory—22 per cent more than it had been allotted by the UN partition. Transjordan took over East Jerusalem and the area known as the West Bank (located on the west bank of the Jordan River). Egypt occupied the coastal plain around the city of Gaza, known as the Gaza Strip. The Palestinian Arab nation that was originally proposed by the UN partition plan, however, was never established.

David Ben-Gurion, Israel's first prime minister, reads the declaration of the founding of the nation of Israel, in Tel Aviv, on May 15, 1948.

THE 1947–1949 WAR

Start date:	November 29, 1947
End date:	February 24, 1949
Duration	453 days
Total deaths (est.)	12,373

Combatants	Deaths
Israel	6,373
Egypt (approx.)	3,000
Syria (approx.)	2,000
Transjordan (approx.)	1,000

CHAPTER 2
THE SUEZ CRISIS AND THE SIX-DAY WAR

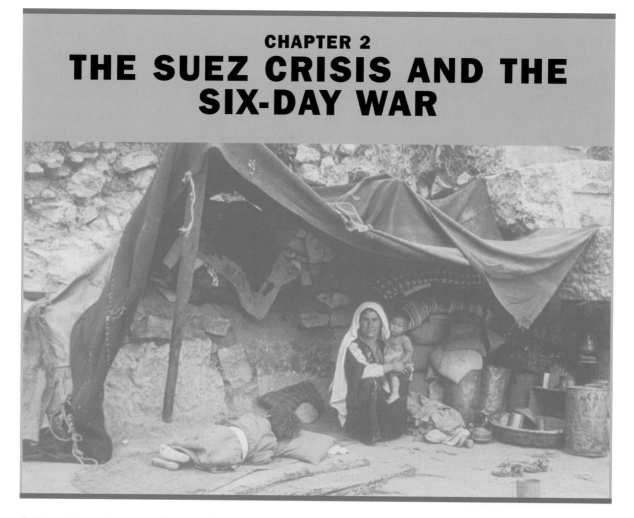

A Palestinian refugee family camps in Amman, Transjordan, in June 1949. Despite a UN resolution recognizing the Palestinians' right to return to their homes, Israel barred refugees from reentering Israel after the 1947–1949 war.

According to UN estimates, the fighting in the 1947–1949 war caused 726,000 Palestinian Arabs to flee Israel and become refugees. About 470,000 moved to the West Bank (controlled by Transjordan, which in 1950 was renamed Jordan) and Gaza Strip (controlled by Egypt); 256,000 went to live in neighboring Arab countries; about 150,000 Palestinian Arabs remained in Israel or returned to their homes in 1949. The reasons for the Palestinian exodus are disputed. Many Palestinian Arabs claim the refugees were deliberately driven out by the Israelis, but Israel insists that Arab government leaders encouraged them to leave.

An uneasy peace existed between Israel and the Arab nations after 1949. Despite the signing of the armistice agreements, none of the Arab countries recognized

Israel's new borders or even its right to exist. Both sides began building up their military forces. The Soviet Union, originally a supporter of Israel, aligned itself with the Arab states and began supplying them with military aid. The United States remained a supporter of Israel, but it did not begin supplying military aid until the 1960s. Israel acquired most of its weaponry from Britain and France.

THE SUEZ WAR The Suez Canal, in Egypt, was built in 1869 by a French company, and at first it was jointly owned by the Egyptian and French governments. The canal, which ran through Egyptian territory, linked the Mediterranean and Red Seas and provided a vital trade route to the east. In 1882,

LEBANON
(13.5%—100,000)

IRAQ→
(0.5%—4,000)

Acre

Safed

Haifa

SYRIA
(10.5%—75,000)

Sea of
Galilee

Tiberias

MEDITERRANEAN
SEA

Beisan

Jordan

THE
WEST
BANK
(38.5%—280,000)

Jaffa

Ramla

☐ AMMAN

☐ JERUSALEM

ISRAEL

TRANSJORDAN
(10%—70,000)

THE GAZA
STRIP
(26%—190,000)

Dead
Sea

Beersheba

0   25 miles
0   25 kilometers

EGYPT
(1%—7,000)

Area from which Palestinians fled,
April–December 1948
Towns with a large Palestinian population
Direction of Palestinian flight
(1%—7,000) Percentage and number of refugees
reaching new areas

debts forced Egypt to sell its share in the canal to Britain.

The canal continued to be jointly controlled by Britain and France until 1956. Early in that year, tensions between Egypt and Israel increased as Egyptians and Palestinians launched a series of border raids against Israel from Gaza. Israel responded with its own attacks. In July, Egyptian leader Gamal Abdel Nasser nationalized (brought under government control) the Suez Canal. Nasser, a supporter of Arab nationalism, did not like European countries having power over Egyptian territory. The tolls he could charge ships passing through the canal would also be a valuable source of revenue for Egypt.

This map shows where Palestinian refugees fled and roughly how many settled in each area. The UN established an agency to care for the refugees. Today, more than 3.7 million Palestinians are registered with the agency.

Nasser arrives in Egypt's capital, Cairo, in August 1956 following his announcement that he had nationalized the Suez Canal.

British paratroopers board an airplane bound for Egypt during the 1956 crisis. Britain and France began bombing Egyptian airfields on October 30 and then sent in troops on November 5.

THE 1956 SINAI CAMPAIGN

Start date:	October 29, 1956
End date:	November 5, 1956
Duration	7 days
Total deaths	2,763

Combatants	Deaths
Israel	231
Egypt	2,500
Britain	22
France	10

By closing the Suez Canal to Israeli shipping and blockading the Straits of Tiran—another key trading route for Israel—Nasser strained relations between Egypt and Israel still further. He also made enemies of Britain and France, because the two countries had major economic and trading interests in the canal. A secret meeting between Israel, Britain, and France took place near Paris. It was agreed that Israel would invade Egypt, and that Britain and France would intervene and ask the Israeli and Egyptian armies to

withdraw from the canal zone. A force of British and French troops would then take control of the canal.

On October 29, 1956, Israeli troops invaded the Gaza Strip and the Sinai Peninsula. They clashed with Egyptian troops but advanced rapidly toward the canal zone. Britain and France, as previously agreed, offered to reoccupy the canal zone and separate the two armies. Nasser refused this request, so Britain and France launched a joint attack. Before the invading forces could reach the canal, however, the United States put pressure on Britain and France to withdraw their troops. The U.S. government was concerned about the damage their action might do to relations with the Arab states. It also feared the possible escalation of the conflict after the Soviet Union threatened to intervene on Egypt's side. The Anglo-French troops were pulled out on December 22, 1956.

Above: French soldiers at Port Said, Egypt. After capturing this city, Anglo-French forces came within 25 miles (40 km) of Suez City before the cease-fire.

Right: The main routes of Israeli forces during the 1956 invasion of Gaza and Sinai. Israeli armored divisions captured almost the entire territory by November 5. The operation took just 100 hours.

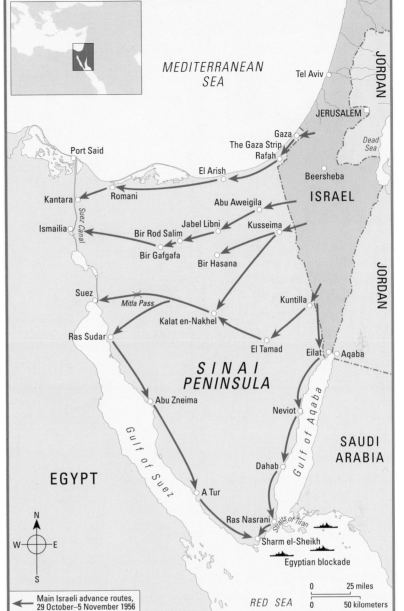

During the conflict, Israel captured both the Sinai Peninsula and the Gaza Strip. In March 1957, however, the UN forced Israel to return to its previous borders. Israel failed to win back its shipping rights in the Suez Canal, but regained the freedom to use the Straits of Tiran. A demilitarized zone, policed by UN forces, was established in the eastern and southern areas of the Sinai, extending from Gaza to Sharm el-Sheikh. The zone provided a buffer between Israel and Egypt.

In August 1963, Israel began putting into effect its National Water Carrier Plan (NWCP), pumping water from the Sea of Galilee to irrigate south and central Israel. Syria, angered by this plan, readied its troops for attack. Israel did likewise. The UN persuaded both sides to pull back from conflict.

During 1964, Arab leaders met at a series of conferences to agree on joint strategies for dealing with Israel. At these conferences, the leaders reached several decisions. They agreed to form the Palestine Liberation Organization (PLO) to represent the cause of Palestinian nationalism and help unite Palestinians wherever they lived; they restated their intention to

Above: Levi Eshkol with his wife, Miriam. Eshkol was Israeli prime minister from 1963 until his death in 1969. His most significant leadership came during the 1967 Six-Day War.

destroy Israel; and they decided to divert the Banias stream—one of the sources of the River Jordan, which feeds the Sea of Galilee—to prevent Israel from carrying out its irrigation plan.

Syria and Lebanon began work on the diversion in early 1967. Israel attempted to block progress by firing on the tractors and earthmoving equipment carrying out the work on the Syrian side of the border. The Syrians responded by shelling Israeli towns in the north. Both sides began carrying out air strikes against targets across the border. As tensions escalated, the Soviet Union informed Syria that Israel was massing troops on the Syrian border in preparation for an invasion. Not knowing that the claim was actually untrue, Syria asked Egypt for help.

"THE DESTRUCTION OF ISRAEL"

On May 15, 1967, Nasser sent Egyptian troops into the Sinai peninsula. Three days later, he asked that UN forces still stationed in the Sinai's demilitarized zone withdraw. UN secretary-general U Thant complied, and Egyptian troops were sent into Sharm el-Sheikh.

Israel's borders between 1949 and 1967. At this time, Israel's Arab neighbors refused to recognize its borders or even its right to exist. Beginning in the mid-1960s, Syrian, Egyptian, and Palestinian border attacks on Israel became more frequent.

On May 21, Nasser closed the Gulf of Aqaba and the Straits of Tiran to Israeli shipping. Israeli prime minister Levi Eshkol interpreted what Nassar had done as an act of aggression against Israel.

Nasser's popularity rose in the Arab world—as in 1956, many Arabs were pleased to see him standing up for Arab interests by confronting the Israelis. On May 27, Nasser announced, "our basic objective will be the destruction of Israel. The Arab people want to fight." PLO Chairman Ahmed Shukhairy echoed these sentiments, saying it would be the PLO's privilege to strike the first blow; they would expel all Zionists from Palestine who had arrived after 1917 and eliminate the nation of Israel. Other Arab nations were persuaded to join Egypt and Syria in committing to war. On May 30, Jordan signed a defense pact with Egypt, and on June 4, Iraq did the same. Iraqi president Rahman Aref declared, "Our goal is to wipe Israel off the map."

The Israeli cabinet was divided on what to do about these threats. Former prime minister David Ben-Gurion preferred to wait, while Moshe Dayan, a veteran soldier of the 1947–1949 war, favored an immediate, preemptive attack on Egypt. The United

" . . . WITH ALL OUR MIGHT"

"We are engaged in defensive fighting on the Egyptian sector, and we shall not engage ourselves in any action against Jordan, unless Jordan attacks us. Should Jordan attack Israel, we shall go against her with all our might."

—A message sent by Israeli prime minister Eshkol to King Hussein of Jordan on the morning of June 5, 1967. That afternoon, under pressure from Egypt, Jordan attacked Israel.

King Hussein of Jordan on a visit to a Royal Air Force base in the United Kingdom in 1966. Jordan signed a mutual defense pact with Egypt in May 1967 and took part in the 1967 conflict with Israel, losing control of the West Bank and Jerusalem in the process.

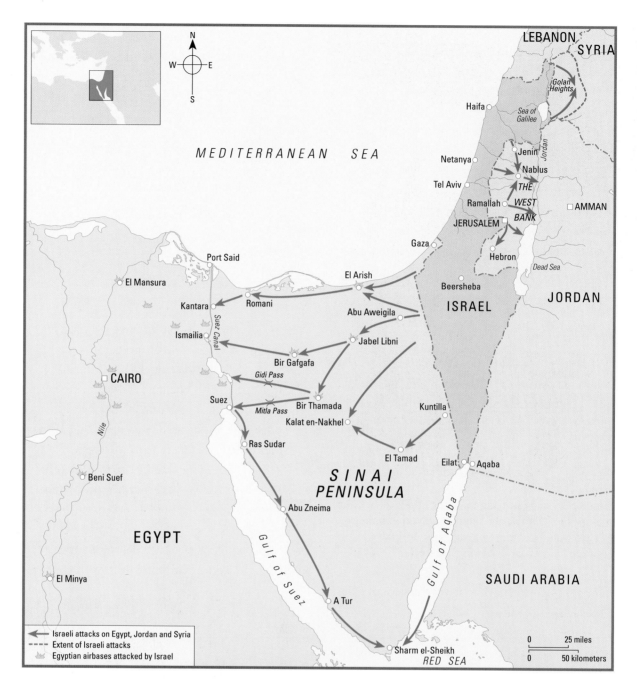

A map showing the Israeli advance on three fronts during the Six-Day War. An important element of Israel's success was its virtual destruction of its enemies' air forces, giving it air superiority throughout the war.

States put pressure on Israel not to attack, but the mood in the cabinet gradually tilted toward aggressive action. Dayan was appointed Minister of Defense on May 31. Menachem Begin, another supporter of war, was also invited to join the government. On June 3, the cabinet learned that the United States would not intervene if Israel went to war. On June 4, 1967, Israel made the decision to attack.

THE SIX-DAY WAR Israel began its offensive at 7.45 am on June 5, 1967, with a surprise attack on the Egyptian air force. Egypt had the best-equipped and most modern of all the Arab air forces, but its airfields were poorly defended, with few antiaircraft guns or armored bunkers. The Israeli jets bombed and strafed the Egyptian planes and runways. In less than three hours they had destroyed virtually the entire air

In addition to destroying many Egyptian aircraft on the ground, the Israelis used penetration bombs to shred the pavement of runways, so that even undamaged planes could not take off.

force on the ground, giving Israel air superiority for the remainder of the war.

Part of the Israeli Defence Force (IDF), consisting of three divisions, began to advance through the Gaza Strip and the Sinai Peninsula, encircling and then defeating a powerful Egyptian force at Abu-Aweigila. When Egyptian Minister of Defense Abdel Amer heard that Abu-Ageila had fallen, he panicked and ordered all units in Sinai to retreat. By June 8, the Israelis had completed their conquest of the Sinai.

Nasser, desperate for help from Jordan, had sent a message on June 5 to its ruler, King Hussein, in which he pretended that the Egyptians were winning their battle with the Israelis. Hussein gave the order to attack, and the Jordanian army began firing on Israeli positions in Jerusalem. Israeli forces counterattacked,

destroying the tiny Jordanian air force and encircling Arab-controlled eastern Jerusalem. On June 6, an Israeli armored brigade captured the West Bank towns of Ramallah and Jenin, and the following day Israeli troops took control of Jerusalem's Old City and the West Bank town of Nablus. By June 8, all of Jerusalem and the West Bank had fallen to Israeli forces.

From the start of the conflict, Syrian artillery had been shelling civilian targets in northern Israel from the Golan Heights, a 3,300-foot (1,000-meter) high plateau on Syria's southwestern frontier with Israel. On the evening of June 5, Israeli jets destroyed two-thirds of the Syrian air force, and forced the remaining third

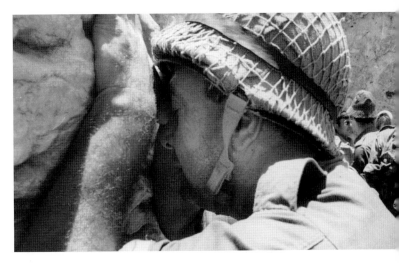

An Israeli soldier at Jerusalem's Wailing Wall—a holy place for Jews—following the Israeli capture of the Old City in 1967.

17

to retreat to distant bases. The Israeli government was divided on whether or not to attempt taking the mountainous Golan Heights, a far more difficult operation than fighting on the flat desert of the Sinai Peninsula. Israeli prime minister Levi Eshkol favored an attack, but Moshe Dayan was concerned about fighting a war on several fronts. As good news poured in from the Sinai Peninsula and the West Bank, however, Dayan warmed to the idea, and he authorized the operation.

Early on the morning of June 9, Israeli jets began bombing Syrian positions on the Golan Heights, and four Israeli brigades secured a base on the plateau for reinforcements. On June 10, the Syrian forces began retreating under heavy bombardment. By the afternoon, Israelis troops

controlled the Golan Heights and were poised to advance on the Syrian capital, Damascus.

At this stage, the Soviet Union, a firm ally of Syria, became alarmed. The Soviet premier, Alexei Kosygin, sent a telegram to U.S. president Lyndon Johnson,

Israeli units advance into Syria on June 10, 1967. During the assault on the Golan Heights, Israel lost 115 soldiers.

THE SIX-DAY WAR

Start date:	June 5, 1967
End date:	June 11, 1967
Duration	6 days
Total deaths (approx.)	19,200

Combatants	Forces (approx.)	Losses
Israel	150,000 troops 1,000 tanks 200 aircraft	776 Not available 46
Egypt	100,000 troops 900 tanks 385 aircraft	10,000 (approx.) Not available 300
Jordan	60,000 troops 300 tanks 24 aircraft	6,000 (approx.) n/a 20
Syria	50,000 troops 200 tanks 97 aircraft	2,500 (approx.) Not available 50

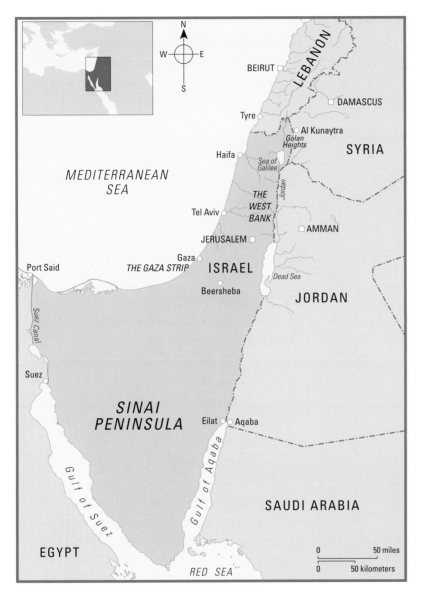

Above: On June 12, 1967, Israeli troops salute their country's flag, now flying over the former Syrian territory of the Golan Heights.

By the end of the 1967 Six-Day War, Israel had expanded its territory from 8,100 square miles (21,000 sq km) to 25,860 square miles (67,000 sq km). It retained these borders until October 1973.

threatening military action against Israel unless it ceased fighting in the next few hours. Both the U.S. government and the UN, concerned that the war might develop into a far more serious confrontation, urged the Israelis to stop their advance. At 6:30 pm on June 10, Israeli commanders ordered a cease-fire.

In the aftermath of the conflict, it was immediately clear that Israel had won a stunning victory. In just six days, Israeli forces had conquered the Gaza Strip, the Sinai Peninsula, the Golan Heights, and the West Bank, more than tripling its territory. Israel had inflicted a

damaging defeat on its enemies and established itself as the dominant military power in the region.

Israel had triumphed despite facing a combined Arab force that was greater in numbers and had more up-to-date weapons and equipment. Israel benefited from better leadership on the battlefield, superior training, and effective tactics of surprise, speed, and air superiority. The Israelis (many of whom had lost family members in the Holocaust of World War II) were also arguably better motivated, since most of them believed they were fighting for the very survival of their nation.

CHAPTER 3
THE OCCUPIED TERRITORIES AND THE RISE OF THE PLO

An Israeli soldier stands guard at the new border with Jordan in June 1967.

Israel's conquests brought their own problems. After the Six-Day War, Israel found itself ruling over more than 750,000 Palestinian Arabs, most of whom were hostile to the Israeli government. Far from bringing Israel a greater sense of security, the 1967 victory only served to increase anti-Israeli sentiment among Arabs in Palestine and elsewhere. In November 1967, the UN gave its own verdict on the war, when the UN Security Council adopted Resolution 242. It called upon Israel to withdraw from territories it seized by force and called upon all nations in the Middle East to live in peace and recognize boundaries established before June 1967.

NEW TERRITORIES Israel initially offered to return all of its new territories, except Jerusalem, in return for peace treaties with its Arab neighbors. Egypt rejected this "land-for-peace" offer on July 18, 1967, and the following day Israel withdrew it. From this point on, any similar Israeli peace initiatives would face strong opposition from religious Zionists in Israel. The Zionists noted that the conquest of the West Bank, Gaza, and the Golan Heights had brought the modern Jewish nation's borders roughly in line with the Biblical land of Israel. They were determined to make these territories a permanent part of Israel and lobbied the Israeli government to annex the territories and allow Jewish settlements to be built there.

In 1977, settlement expansion became official government policy, and increasing numbers of Jewish settlers made their homes in these areas. By 2003, 220,000 Jews had settled in the West Bank and Gaza, and an additional 200,000 had moved into areas of Jerusalem conquered in 1967. Some 15,000 Jews have settled in the Golan Heights, which Israel formally

RESOLUTION 242

In its Resolution 242, the UN Security Council called for: *"(i) Withdrawal of Israeli armed forces from territories occupied in the recent conflict; (ii) Termination of all claims or states of belligerency [being at war] and respect for and acknowledgement of the sovereignty, territorial integrity and political independence of every State in the area and their right to live in peace within secure and recognized boundaries free from threats or acts of force . . . "*

Refugees cross between Jordan and Israel in 1967. Today, over half of the three million Palestinians in the West Bank and Gaza are refugees.

Above: Palestinian cities and Jewish settlements in the West Bank and Gaza Strip.

annexed from Syria in 1981. These settlements are in breach of UN Resolution 242 and have been a source of great anger and resentment for the Palestinian Arabs living in the occupied territories. Israel insists it has not broken international law with regard to the West Bank and Gaza Strip because they were not part of the sovereign territory of any nation when Israel took them over. The territories were formerly part of the British Mandate, and as part of the armistice agreement at the end of the 1947–1949 war, Egypt annexed Gaza and Jordan annexed the West Bank. The territories, however, were never internationally recognized as permanent parts of those countries. Therefore, Israel argues, it is not a foreign occupier. Instead, it is a legal administrator of territories whose precise status remains to be determined.

Beginning in June 1967, Israel established a military administration to govern the Palestinians living in the West Bank and the Gaza Strip, which became known collectively as the occupied territories. The Israelis granted Palestinians living in these territories freedom of worship, but in order to enforce security and counterterrorism there, restrictions were placed on the Palestinian residents' freedom of movement and freedom of the press. The Israeli authorities imposed curfews and closed roads, schools, and community institutions. Houses of suspected terrorists were demolished, and hundreds of Palestinians, accused of terrorist offenses, were deported to Jordan or Lebanon or imprisoned.

JERUSALEM Jerusalem has always had a special status because of its importance as a holy place to Jews, Muslims, and Christians. The UN partition plan of

1947 advised that Jerusalem become an international city. The armistice agreed between Israel and Jordan after the 1947–1949 war split the city in two: Israel took control of West Jerusalem while Jordan occupied East Jerusalem. East Jerusalem included the old walled city that contains religious sites important to Jews, Muslims, and Christians. The city remained divided until 1967, when Israel captured East Jerusalem from Jordan and then annexed it soon afterward.

Unlike Gaza and the West Bank, which were ruled by military administrations, Arab East Jerusalem was governed by Israeli civil law. Israeli authorities redrew Jerusalem's boundaries, extending them northward and southward. Large Israeli settlements were established around the northern, eastern, and southern boundaries of the city, creating a physical barrier between the Palestinian Arabs in East Jerusalem and their fellow Arabs living elsewhere in

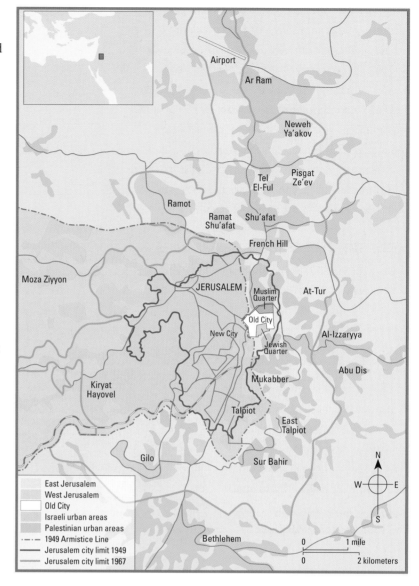

East Jerusalem
West Jerusalem
Old City
Israeli urban areas
Palestinian urban areas
1949 Armistice Line
Jerusalem city limit 1949
Jerusalem city limit 1967

Above: Jerusalem since the Israeli conquest of 1967. Israel annexed 4 square miles (10 sq km) of Jordanian Jerusalem and 40 sq miles (103 sq km) of the nearby West Bank, renaming the entire area East Jerusalem.

Left: Jews pray at the Wailing Wall in Jerusalem in 1973. Also known as the Western Wall, it is all that remains of the Jerusalem Temple, which the Romans destroyed in the first century A.D. Jews regard it as the holiest place on earth.

the West Bank. In 1980, Israel's parliament passed a law making its annexation of Jerusalem official.

Jerusalem remains one of the most problematic issues in the Arab-Israeli conflict. Neither Israel nor the Palestinians agree with the UN plan to make Jerusalem an international city. Israel sees Jerusalem—the capital of ancient Israel—as its "eternal capital," and it is unlikely that an Israeli government would ever voluntarily give it up. Arabs regard East Jerusalem as part of the occupied West Bank, and they want it to be the capital of a future Palestinian nation.

THE CHANGING BALANCE OF POPULATION IN JERUSALEM

	Jews	Arabs
1948	100,000	65,000
1967	195,700	65,763
1984	346,700	126,100
1993	401,000	155,000
2000	454,600	215,400

An Arab Muslim passes two orthodox Jews in a Jerusalem street. On June 27, 1967, the Israeli parliament voted to give people of all religions free access to Jerusalem's holy sites.

RISE OF THE PLO The Palestine Liberation Organization, or PLO, was founded in Egypt in 1964 to represent the large numbers of Palestinian Arabs living as refugees in Syria, Jordan, and Egypt. In its early years, the organization was controlled by the Arab nations that hoped to use it to advance their interests in the region. After the Six-Day War, however, many Palestinian Arabs lost faith in the Arab regimes and began to build their own nationalist movements. One of these groups, called Fatah and led by a young Palestinian named Yasser Arafat, took over the PLO in 1967.

The PLO, now independent of the Arab regimes, became an umbrella organization for about eight different nationalist groups, each with their own views of how to achieve the ultimate goal of a Palestinian state. Arafat, as leader of the largest group, Fatah, became chairman of the PLO in 1969. The other major factions included the Popular Front for the Liberation of Palestine (PFLP), the Democratic Front for the Liberation of Palestine (DFLP), and the Palestine People's Party (PPP). Despite their various

differences, most members of these groups—and the majority of Palestinians—regarded the PLO as their representative.

After the Six-Day War, some 400,000 Palestinians fled the West Bank for Jordan, where the PLO regrouped and decided to adopt terrorist tactics. In 1968, it began a campaign of hijackings and border raids into Israel from Jordan and Syria. On one occasion, in March of 1968, a Jordanian-PLO force managed to inflict a rare defeat on Israeli troops in the town of Karameh in Jordan. The Israeli assault was launched after a terrorist attack left two Jewish schoolchildren dead. The Israelis were driven back by Palestinian guerrillas supported by Jordanian troops and artillery. This victory gave Arafat worldwide fame and enabled him to recruit many more Palestinians to his cause.

One of the airliners blown up by the PFLP at Dawson's Field, Jordan, in 1970. This terrorism led to the expulsion of the PLO from Jordan.

In 1970, one of the PLO factions, the PFLP, blew up three passenger planes at Dawson's Field, a military airport in Jordan. By this time, the increasingly violent activities of the PLO were putting pressure on Jordan's King Hussein, who felt that he was losing control of his own country. In 1970 and 1971, the Jordanian army forced the PLO out of Jordan and into southern Lebanon. From its new base, the PLO continued to raid and shell northern Israel.

During the 1970s, however, the PLO began to alter its strategy. Concerned about its image as a terrorist organization, it began to seek international legitimacy as a government-in-exile. At the Arab League conference in Morocco in 1974, the PLO was officially recognized by the Arab peoples as the representative organization of the Palestinians, and in November of that year, Arafat was invited to address the UN General Assembly. The UN then granted the PLO observer status, which entitled it to participate as an observer in all the sessions and debates of the General Assembly. To Israel's discomfort, Arafat had changed the image of the PLO from a group of ruthless terrorists to an internationally respected movement.

Jordanian premier Abdel Min'em Rifa'i with PLO leader Yasser Arafat (left) in 1969.

"SOMETHING HAD TO BE DONE . . . "

"The humiliation of having aircraft flown into Jordan and innocent passengers being whisked away to various parts of the country, and being unable to do anything about it, and having aircraft blown up, was something that questioned whether Jordan really existed. Well, that was the limit. As far as I was concerned, something had to be done—and done quickly.'

—King Hussein of Jordan on his decision to expel the PLO

THE OCCUPIED TERRITORIES AND THE RISE OF THE PLO

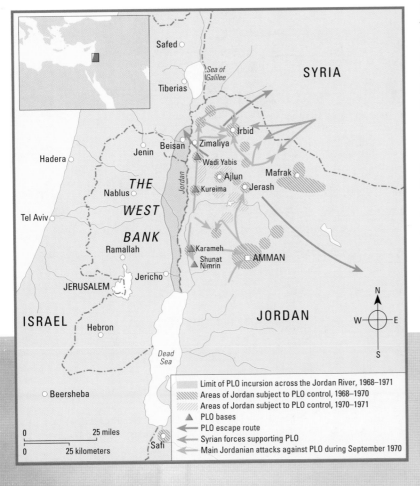

Left: The conflict between the PLO and Jordanian forces erupted in June 1970. At one stage early in the battle, a Syrian tank force moved into northern Jordan to support the PLO but was forced to retreat.

Below: Palestinian guerrillas, known as the fedayeen, patrol the streets of Amman during the PLO-Jordanian conflict. A cease-fire came into force in September 1970, but sporadic fighting continued until Jordanian forces won a decisive victory in July 1971.

Limit of PLO incursion across the Jordan River, 1968–1971
Areas of Jordan subject to PLO control, 1968–1970
Areas of Jordan subject to PLO control, 1970–1971
▲ PLO bases
← PLO escape route
← Syrian forces supporting PLO
← Main Jordanian attacks against PLO during September 1970

CHAPTER 4

THE YOM KIPPUR WAR AND CAMP DAVID

Above: Artillery fire against Israel during the Yom Kippur War. The Egyptian-Syrian attack had military and financial support from other Arab nations.

Below: Soviet premier Leonid Brezhnev greets Anwar Sadat in Moscow in 1971. Sadat was seeking Soviet military support for Egypt.

In 1968, Egypt began engaging in a series of low-level but persistent attacks against Israel in the Sinai Peninsula, with the goal of wearing down Israeli forces. The cross-border confrontations grew increasingly intense until, under U.S. pressure, both sides signed a cease-fire in August 1970 and declared their acceptance of UN Resolution 242. Shortly afterward, Egyptian leader Nasser died. He was replaced by a new leader, Anwar Sadat.

Unlike his predecessor, Sadat was genuinely interested in making peace with Israel. In February 1971, he announced that if Israel partially withdrew its forces from the Sinai, Egypt would reopen the Suez Canal and sign a peace agreement with Israel. By this time, Israel had a new prime minister, Golda Meir, who refused the Egyptian offer, despite pressure from the United States to accept. Over the next two years, further offers of peace were also turned down. Israel, now receiving U.S. military aid, believed it was in a strong position in relation to Egypt, whose forces had yet to recover their pre-1967 strength.

Israeli plans to build a Mediterranean port at Rafah in the Sinai, and its talk of creating settlements there, worried Sadat. He thought that the only way to

The lines of attack and counterattack during the Yom Kippur War. For the first four days of the conflict, Egypt and Syria made strong headway against surprised Israeli defenses. After three weeks of fighting, however, the Israeli Defense Force (IDF) was able to push enemy forces back beyond their original lines.

recover this territory, and to lift Egypt's standing in the Arab world, would be to stage an attack on Israel.

THE OCTOBER WAR On the afternoon of October 6, 1973, Egypt and Syria launched a joint invasion of Israel, code-named Operation Badr. They chose the day deliberately: it was Yom Kippur, or the Day of Atonement, the holiest day in the Jewish calendar, and the Israelis were caught completely by

AIR ATTACK

"It was one o'clock in the afternoon, and I was driving my jeep to meet my commander. Suddenly I saw planes. I was very surprised. The Israeli air force flying on Yom Kippur! . . . [then] I understood we were in a war."

—General Amram Mitzna, Armored Corps, IDF

surprise. Golda Meir and Defense Minister Moshe Dayan had believed that their forces in the Sinai peninsula were sufficient to deter any attack, and they dismissed intelligence reports that enemy soldiers were massing on the border preparing to invade.

Huge numbers of Egyptian troops poured across the Suez Canal virtually unopposed and established a beachhead. A tiny force of Israelis manning the outposts along the canal were destroyed after offering limited resistance. Within days, Egyptian forces had successfully reconquered the entire western bank of the Sinai peninsula. Israel's counterattacks on land and in the air were successfully repelled by Egypt's new Soviet-made antitank and antiaircraft missiles. These missiles were neutralized only after Egyptian radar stations (which directed their strikes) were destroyed.

To the north, meanwhile, Israeli defenses that included just 170 tanks were overrun by far greater Syrian forces (including 1,500 tanks and 1,000 artillery pieces) which penetrated deep into the Golan Heights and came within sight of the Sea of Galilee in northern

Israel. During three days of desperate fighting, Israel's 7th Brigade managed to hold a line of rocky hills defending the northern side of their headquarters in Nafah (see page 27). The Syrians, however, came very close to capturing Nafah from the south after destroying the Israeli "Barak" armored brigade. Israeli reserve forces arrived in time to prevent the capture of Nafah, and they swiftly counterattacked.

THE OCTOBER WAR

Start date:	October 6, 1973
End date:	October 22, 1973
Duration	16 days
Deaths per day	781
Total deaths (approx)	14,188

Combatants	Deaths
Israel	2,688
Egypt	8,500 (approx)
Syria	3,000 (approx)

An Israeli armored column advances into Syria on October 17, 1973. That day, Arab nations declared an oil embargo against the United States and other countries for supporting Israel, which led to higher gas prices.

By October 11, they had reversed the Syrian gains, advancing to within artillery range of the Syrian capital, Damascus, just 25 miles (40 km) away.

On the night of October 16 and 17, General Ariel Sharon, commanding an Israeli division in the Sinai, disobeyed orders from his more cautious superiors and crossed to the Egyptian side of the canal, where he established a bridgehead between the Egyptian second and third armies. Israeli forces were able to cut off supplies to the Egyptian third army fighting in the peninsula, and they came within 60 miles (100 km)

of Cairo, Egypt's capital city. Israeli attempts to capture Suez City, however, ended in failure. Under U.S. and Soviet pressure, Egypt and Israel agreed to a cease-fire on October 20. Two days later, Israel and Syria agreed to a cease-fire, based on a return to pre-war borders.

After being caught so badly off guard, Israeli forces managed a rapid recovery and recaptured nearly all the territory they had won in 1967. Nevertheless, the war was a great shock to the Israelis, and losses had been heavy. They had underestimated the strength of their enemies and had come very close to defeat. The Israeli government's lack of preparedness led to the resignation of Golda Meir and Moshe Dayan.

Occasional clashes continued across the cease-fire lines in the Sinai and the Golan Heights, but tensions were eased on March 5, 1974, when Israeli forces withdrew from the west bank of the Suez

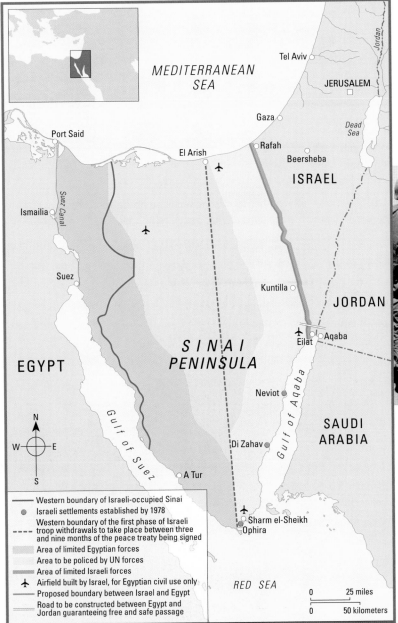

Western boundary of Israeli-occupied Sinai
● Israeli settlements established by 1978
- - - Western boundary of the first phase of Israeli troop withdrawals to take place between three and nine months of the peace treaty being signed
Area of limited Egyptian forces
Area to be policed by UN forces
Area of limited Israeli forces
✈ Airfield built by Israel, for Egyptian civil use only
Proposed boundary between Israel and Egypt
Road to be constructed between Egypt and Jordan guaranteeing free and safe passage

Above: Following the end of the conflict, blindfolded Egyptian prisoners of war are led back to the western side of the Suez Canal so they can return home.

Left: The Sinai boundary changes agreed to at Camp David (see p. 30) in September 1978. Under the agreement, the Sinai would be returned to Egypt but part of the territory would be policed by the UN as a security measure.

Begin (left), Carter (center), and Sadat meet at Camp David in September 1978. The U.S. president formed a relationship of friendship and mutual trust with Sadat but found it harder to work with Begin.

Canal, and Egypt took back control. On May 31, 1974, Syria and Israel signed a disengagement agreement, and a UN peacekeeping force was established in the Golan Heights. U.S. secretary of state Henry Kissinger tried to negotiate an Arab-Israeli peace settlement by encouraging Israel to withdraw partly from the Sinai and the Golan Heights, but he failed. The United States was successful, however, in achieving a limited agreement between Egypt and Israel in September 1975 in which Israel withdrew most of its forces from the Sinai, and a UN-policed buffer zone was introduced between Egyptian and Israeli forces.

In November 1977, Sadat visited Jerusalem in an effort to secure peace between Egypt and Israel. He offered the Israelis permanent peace and recognition of Israeli sovereignty if Israel would withdraw from the occupied territories, including Arab Jerusalem, and agree to the establishment of a Palestinian nation. Israeli prime minister Menachem Begin could not accept such an agreement, but he did offer limited self-rule for the Palestinians in the West Bank and Gaza.

CAMP DAVID In September 1978, U.S. president Jimmy Carter invited Sadat and Begin to the Camp David presidential retreat in Maryland. Following 12 days of secret and often hostile discussions, two agreements were signed. The first agreement dealt with Egypt-Israel relations: both countries recognized each other, and the Sinai was returned to Egypt. This agreement led to the Egypt-Israel Peace Treaty—the first between Israel and an Arab nation—signed in March 1979. Israel completed its withdrawal from the Sinai Peninsula in 1982.

The second agreement attempted to solve the Palestinian problem. It proposed giving Palestinians

TOUGH TALKING

"I want you to understand that my right eye will fall out, my right hand will fall off, before I sign a single scrap of paper permitting the dismantling of a single Jewish settlement."

—Menachem Begin, speaking to U.S. national security advisor Zbigniew Brzezinski at Camp David about Jewish settlements in the Sinai

Map legend:
⭐ Main PLO terrorist attacks in Israel, 1976–1978
▨ Area occupied by Israeli forces, 15 March–13 June 1978

LEBANON
BEIRUT
Sidon
MEDITERRANEAN SEA
Tyre
Litani
DAMASCUS
SYRIA
Nahariya
6 November 1977, 2 killed
Golan Heights
Haifa
Sea of Galilee
11 March 1978, 39 killed
Jordan
Tel Aviv
THE WEST BANK
AMMAN
JERUSALEM
1976, 8 killed
Gaza
THE GAZA STRIP
JORDAN
Dead Sea
Beersheba
ISRAEL
0   50 miles
0   50 kilometers
SINAI
Eilat   Aqaba

This map shows PLO attacks on Israel (1976–1978) and Operation Litani, Israel's occupation of southern Lebanon (March–June 1978) that was undertaken in an attempt to strike back at the PLO.

occupied territories or the establishment of an independent Palestinian state. Israel also made the agreement more difficult to achieve by continuing to build new settlements in these areas.

OPERATION LITANI

Another reason for the failure to achieve an Israeli-Palestinian peace agreement in 1978 was the growing conflict on Israel's northern border with Lebanon. The arrival of the PLO in Lebanon in 1971, after its expulsion from Jordan, had caused tensions within the different ethnic communities of Lebanon—Muslim, Christian, and Druze. Each sect had its own private army, and there were frequent clashes between PLO fighters and Christian militias in the capital city, Beirut. These clashes led to a full-scale civil war beginning in 1975.

In 1976, PLO forces based in southern Lebanon began engaging in a number of terrorist attacks on Israeli forces both in the occupied territories and in Israel. Following a PLO attack on a bus north of Tel Aviv that caused heavy casualties, Israel decided to attack PLO bases in Lebanon.

The invasion of southern Lebanon, known as Operation Litani, took place in March 1978. Israeli forces occupied most of the area south of the Litani River, which had been used as a base for anti-Israeli attacks. The UN Security Council responded by passing Resolution 425 calling for the immediate withdrawal of Israeli forces, and a UN peacekeeping force was set up in Lebanon. Israeli forces withdrew in June 1978, handing over positions along the border to a pro-Israeli force, a group of Lebanese Christian militiamen known as the South Lebanon Army. Israel was thus able to maintain a 12-mile (20-km) wide security zone to protect itself from cross-border attacks.

in the occupied territories autonomy (self-rule) for a five-year period, after which time the final status of the occupied territories would be decided. This agreement was rejected by the PLO and Arab nations because it did not guarantee full Israeli withdrawal from the

Left: A street battle in Beirut during the civil war in Lebanon. Palestinian forces joined Lebanese Muslim factions in a fight against Christian militias based in east Beirut.

CHAPTER 5
THE WAR IN LEBANON AND THE INTIFADA

Ariel Sharon, a key planner behind Operation Peace for Galilee, went beyond the original idea to attack PLO strongholds in southern Lebanon and launched a full-scale assault on Beirut.

Despite Operation Litani and the establishment of a security zone, towns in Galilee in northern Israel continued to suffer attacks from PLO forces in southern Lebanon. To add to Israel's anxiety, Syria had become involved in Lebanon. In 1976, Syrian forces had moved in at the request of one of the factions fighting the civil war, a Christian sect called the Maronites. Syria had used this involvement as an opportunity to take over part of Lebanon for itself.

Tensions between Syria and Israel escalated in April 1982, when Syria began positioning antiaircraft missile batteries in Lebanon's Bekaa Valley. Israel saw the missiles as a threat to its air reconnaissance activities over Lebanon. The Israeli government decided that another invasion of Lebanon was necessary to destroy both the PLO bases and the Syrian missile batteries. Israel also wanted to form

a partnership with the Maronite Christians, because a Maronite government in Lebanon would—the Israelis hoped—be able to rid Lebanon of its Palestinian and Syrian elements. By mid-1977, the Maronites had begun to fear the growing dominance of their former allies, the Syrians, who were behaving increasingly like an army of occupation. The Maronite leaders were happy to form a new allegiance with Israel, the only force in the region powerful enough to confront Syria.

OPERATION PEACE FOR GALILEE

On June 3, 1982, an attempt was made to assassinate the Israeli ambassador in London. The Palestine National Liberation Movement—a rival organization to the PLO—was responsible, but the Israelis now had the excuse they were looking for to begin their invasion of Lebanon, which they named Operation Peace for Galilee. The invasion, planned by Defense Minister Ariel Sharon and Chief of Staff Rafael Eitan, began on June 6, 1982. The Israeli army advanced into Lebanon, quickly overrunning PLO positions in the south, and reached the outskirts of Beirut, Lebanon's capital and the headquarters of the PLO, by June 8 .

On June 9 and 10, the Israeli Air Force (IAF) attacked and destroyed the 19 Syrian missile batteries and their radar sites in the Bekaa Valley. The Syrian Air Force counterattacked, and a massive air battle took place, involving about 200 planes. The IAF inflicted a heavy defeat on the Syrians, who suffered from a lack of ground support, destroying at least

THE ISRAELI INVASION OF LEBANON

Start date:	June 6, 1982
End date:	August 21, 1982
Duration:	77 days
Total deaths:	3,968

Combatants	Deaths
Israel	368
PLO forces	3,000
Syria	600

Source: Martin Gilbert

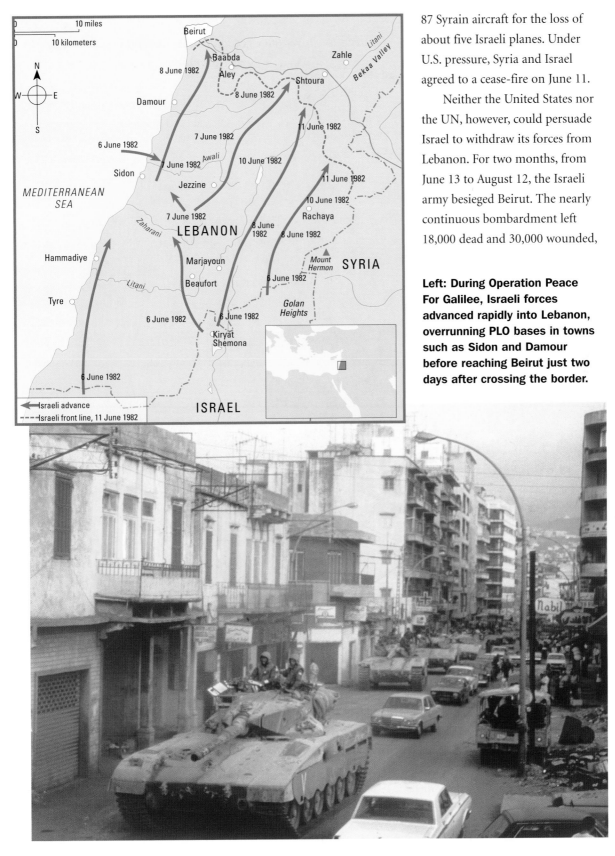

87 Syrain aircraft for the loss of about five Israeli planes. Under U.S. pressure, Syria and Israel agreed to a cease-fire on June 11.

Neither the United States nor the UN, however, could persuade Israel to withdraw its forces from Lebanon. For two months, from June 13 to August 12, the Israeli army besieged Beirut. The nearly continuous bombardment left 18,000 dead and 30,000 wounded,

Left: During Operation Peace For Galilee, Israeli forces advanced rapidly into Lebanon, overrunning PLO bases in towns such as Sidon and Damour before reaching Beirut just two days after crossing the border.

An Israeli tank on the streets of Beirut during the 1982 war. The Israelis would sometimes strike at civilian targets if they had intelligence that PLO arms and munitions were hidden there.

Above: An Israeli military convoy moves south across the Lebanese border as part of the Israeli withdrawal from Lebanon in 1985.

most of the casualties being civilians. Israel insisted that it would only end the siege when the 9,000-strong PLO force surrendered or left Lebanon, together with the Syrian forces stationed in Beirut. In August, U.S. mediators succeeded in establishing a cease–fire and the evacuation of PLO fighters from Lebanon. The evacuation began on August 21. The PLO members moved to a number of different Arab countries, and the PLO leadership eventually settled into a new base in Tunisia.

Israel had succeeded in removing the PLO from Beirut but had failed to neutralize the threat

Right: On September 3, 1983, Israeli troops in Lebanon pulled back to the Awali River as part of a staged withdrawal of Israel's military presence in Lebanon.

RESPONSIBILITY

"It was only my allies, the Lebanese, who pushed me into leaving Beirut. Only when they told me, 'Please, Arafat, this is enough . . . what are you waiting for, Abu Ammar? Look, we are facing death from shelling and bombing from the sea, the land, the air . . . ' that I began to feel responsible for killing their children."

—PLO leader Yasser Arafat

An Israeli soldier in Sidon, southern Lebanon. By 1984, heavy casualty rates and a lack of clear goals led many Israelis to question the wisdom of the invasion.

from Syria, which continued to control 35 per cent of Lebanon. Although the Maronite Lebanese government was sympathetic to Israel, it was too weak to prevent continuing attacks on Israel by Syrian-backed Lebanese and Palestinian factions. A peace treaty between Lebanon and Israel that called for Syrian troop withdrawals was signed in May 1983, but it was cancelled by the Lebanese in March 1984, under pressure from Syria.

Many people in Israel began to see the Lebanese invasion as a costly mistake. Over 300 Israelis had died in the operation, but hostile elements in Lebanon had not been defeated. In addition, Israel's international standing had been damaged by the invasion, which many saw as an unjustifiable act of aggression. There were antiwar demonstrations in Israel that demanded withdrawal. In September 1983, Israeli forces withdrew as far as the Awali River. In June 1985, they withdrew from most of Lebanon but maintained a 5-mile (8-km) wide security zone

Palestinians throw rocks at Israeli tanks and soldiers in Ramallah on the West Bank in May 1988. The PLO later claimed to have organized the intifada, but it was most likely a spontaneous uprising.

along the border that was policed by Israeli troops and members of the Maronite South Lebanon Army. Israeli forces withdrew completely from Lebanon in May 2000.

THE INTIFADA By the mid-1980s, the Palestinians' plight had aroused sympathy around the world, but their situation had remained largely unchanged since 1967. The Israeli occupation of the West Bank and Gaza Strip seemed as if it would continue indefinitely, new Israeli settlements were being built, and PLO leaders—now based in Tunisia—appeared powerless. The anger felt by many Palestinians about their situation was ready to boil over.

On December 8, 1987, an Israeli vehicle crashed into a car filled with Arabs waiting at a road block in Gaza. Four of the Arabs were killed. By nightfall, a rumor had spread through Jabalya—the largest refugee camp in Gaza— that this "accident" had been a revenge attack for a previous killing. This rumor sparked a mass uprising that came to be known as the *Intifada*, which means "shaking off" in Arabic. Riots in Jabalya

IMPACT OF THE INTIFADA

Year	Palestinians killed by Israeli security forces	Palestinians killed by Israeli civilians	Israeli civilians killed by Palestinians	Israeli security forces personnel killed by Palestinians
1987 (Dec. 9–31)	22	0	0	0
1988	290	20	8	4
1989	286	19	20	11
1990	126	19	17	5
1991	96	8	14	5
1992	136	2	19	15
1993 (to Sep 13)	131	7	22	20
TOTAL	**1,087**	**75**	**100**	**60**

(Source: www.btselem.org/English/Statistics/Total_Casualties.asp)

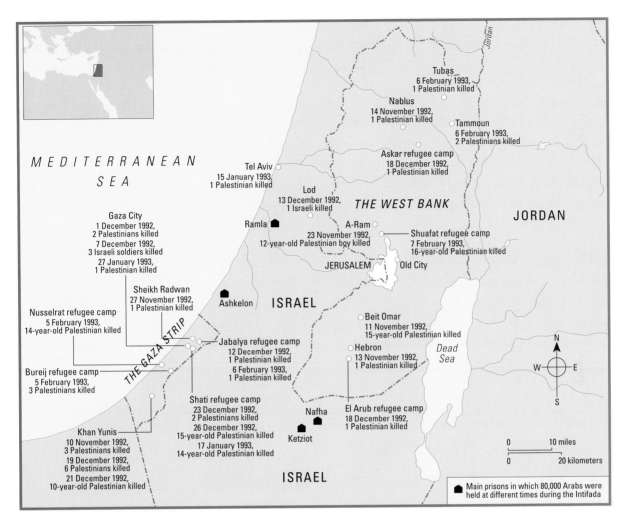

The locations of intifada-related killings reported between November 1992 and February 1993, when the violence intensified. As the intifada progressed, the Palestinians' weapons changed from rocks to gasoline bombs, grenades, guns, and explosives.

soon spread to Gaza City, Nablus on the West Bank, and even into Jerusalem.

Unlike previous riots, the Palestinians were not deterred by the arrival of Israeli troops and armored personnel carriers but continued demonstrating and throwing bottles and stones. Gaza City streets were barricaded with stones and burning tires, fiercely defended by Palestinian youths. Israeli forces hit back, killing 26 Palestinians and injuring 320. By December 20, 1987, some order had been restored with the introduction of road blocks, body searches, and identity cards, but it was clear that the uprising had not been defeated.

Although this first phase of the intifada was spontaneous, the next phase was planned. It was organized by different PLO groups—Fatah, the PFLP, the DFLP, and the PPP—under the overall control of the United National Leadership of the Uprising

(UNLU). Thousands of Palestinians were involved, including many who had no previous experience of resistance, such as women and children. The intifada involved different forms of resistance, including both violence and civil disobedience. In addition to stone-throwing and the building of barricades, there were demonstrations, strikes, boycotts of Israeli products, and mass refusal to pay taxes.

The Israelis attempted to smash the intifada with brute force. Between 1987 and 1991, Israeli forces killed over 1,000 Palestinians and imprisoned about 10,000. By 1990, most UNLU leaders had been either killed or arrested, and the intifada had begun to run out of momentum. The uprising continued, however, until September 1993.

The intifada failed in its main goal of bringing the Israeli occupation to an end. It succeeded, however, in refocusing international attention on the Palestinian liberation struggle. It also shifted political power away from the PLO leadership in Tunisia—which had not started the uprising or played a significant part in its operation—and toward Palestinian groups based in the occupied territories.

THE GULF WAR

On August 2, 1990, Iraq invaded Kuwait, a small oil-rich country on its southern border. This act of aggression was widely condemned worldwide. A coalition of countries led by the United States was formed, and this coalition threatened to take military action against Iraq unless it withdrew. The coalition included a number of Arab countries, including Saudi Arabia and Egypt. A large U.S. military force began gathering in the Persian Gulf.

In a cunning move, Iraqi leader Saddam Hussein attempted to split the coalition by linking Iraq's action to Israel's occupation of the West Bank and Gaza. He declared that he would only withdraw from Kuwait after Israel withdrew from the territories it had seized. In these circumstances, the PLO leadership felt it had no choice but to support Iraq. Hussein and PLO leader Arafat released a joint statement, declaring they were united in their struggle against Israeli occupation and U.S. intervention in the Gulf. Despite this provocation, Arab nations stood firm with the coalition, and Saudi Arabia and other Gulf nations threw out a number of Palestinian activists. The PLO lost some international support for its stance. Palestinians, however, were inspired by Saddam Hussein's boast, and many saw him as a possible liberator of their people.

On January 16, 1991, the UN-imposed deadline for Iraqi withdrawal from Kuwait expired, and the coalition forces unleashed Operation Desert Storm—the removal of Iraqi forces from Kuwait by force. The occupation of Kuwait lasted just seven months before the coalition drove out the Iraqis. During the fighting, Israeli citizens were issued gas masks because of the danger from Iraqi chemical weapons.

The remains of an Iraqi Scud shot down by a Patriot missile near Riyadh, Saudi Arabia. During the Gulf War, Iraq fired 46 Scuds at Saudi Arabia and 40 Scuds at Israel.

U.S. fighter jets fly over burning Kuwait oil fields during the Gulf War. Iraqi soldiers set fire to many of the oil wells in late February 1991.

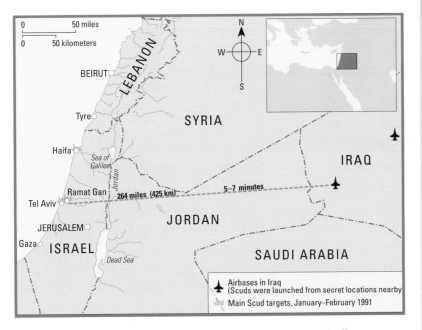

This map shows the main Israeli targets of Iraq's Scud missile campaign in January and February 1991 and the launch sites in Iraq. Many Scuds were shot down by U.S.-supplied Patriot missiles.

POPULAR RIOT

"It was clear that this uprising [the 1987-1993 intifada] was on a new scale, and that these people were not 'terrorists,' but the population itself. There was a real threat that they might overwhelm the Israeli soldiers who were there in very small numbers. If they did, this would leave the soldiers with only two possibilities: to run away, or to shoot. . . . We were not technically prepared to deal with a violent popular riot on this scale."

—Ehud Barak, Israeli Deputy Chief of Staff

In addition, parts of the occupied territories were placed under curfew in case the war sparked unrest in the Palestinian community.

On January 17, Iraq launched eight Scud missiles into Israel, hitting parts of Tel Aviv and Haifa. Saddam Hussein's tactic was to draw Israel into the conflict, knowing that Arab countries would find it hard, if not impossible, to fight alongside Israel against another Arab nation. The U.S. government gave Israel Patriot surface-to-air missiles to shoot down the Scuds but urged Israel not to respond. The Scud attacks increased popular Palestinian support for Saddam, the first Arab leader to match words with actions and attack Israel's heartland. Israel suffered further Scud strikes but did not hit back, and the nation won a lot of international sympathy for its restraint.

CHAPTER 6
THE PEACE PROCESS

When he became prime minister in 1988, Yitzhak Shamir had a reputation as a hard-liner, having opposed the 1979 peace treaty with Egypt. Yet he was prepared to let the Israeli government take part in the 1991 Madrid peace talks.

By November 1988, the intifada was almost a year old, yet the Palestinians seemed no farther along the road toward independence. Palestinian activists in the occupied territories asked the PLO leadership in Tunisia to give a clearer political framework to their struggle. In response, the PLO made a number of key decisions. It agreed to recognize the state of Israel; it declared an independent Palestinian state in the West Bank and the Gaza Strip; and it renounced terrorism.

Israel failed to respond to this gesture. To Israel, the PLO remained a terrorist organization with which it refused to negotiate. Two events in 1991, however, served to help the cause of peace. First, with the collapse of the Soviet Union, Arab states such as Syria and Egypt lost a key supporter, and so they had to be more accommodating in their dealings with Israel's most powerful ally, the United States. Second, after the Gulf War the United States was grateful for the support of the Arab states, and in return was willing to promote a settlement to the Arab-Israeli conflict, if necessary by putting pressure on Israel.

THE MADRID CONFERENCE In October 1991, the United States organized a peace conference in Madrid, Spain, with the goal of resolving the long-running conflict. Israel, Syria, Lebanon, Jordan, and the Palestinians were invited. It was the first time Israel had entered into direct negotiations with any of these nations. Israeli prime minister Yitzhak Shamir insisted that the PLO must be left out of the talks, so the Palestinians were represented by a delegation from the occupied territories. The delegation, however, was guided by PLO leaders staying in nearby hotels.

The talks consisted of both bilateral negotiations between Israel and each Arab state and multilateral negotiations dealing with issues concerning all of the Middle East, such as water supplies, arms control, economic development, and refugees. The discussions that began in Madrid continued over the next three years in different places around the world. The Israel-Jordan talks resulted in the signing of a peace treaty between the two nations in October 1994.

Despite numerous meetings between the Israeli and Palestinian delegations at Madrid, little progress was made. Further talks were held in Washington, D.C., in mid-1992, following the election of a new Israeli government headed by Yitzhak Rabin. By December, however, these talks had also become

"ENOUGH"

"We who have come from a land where parents bury their children, we who have fought against you, the Palestinians, say to you today in a loud and clear voice, enough of bloodshed and tears. Enough."
—Israeli prime minister Yitzhak Rabin before the signing of the Oslo Accords, September 13, 1993

Above: The agreed boundary between Israel and Jordan following the 1994 peace treaty. The treaty confirmed that each country could obtain their fair share of water from the Jordan River.

The fall of the Berlin Wall (right) on November 9, 1989, and the subsequent end of the Cold War marked the beginning of a new drive toward peace in the Middle East. The United States and Russia, former Cold War rivals, put pressure on Israel and the Arab nations to negotiate.

bogged down. The slow pace of negotiations made people in the occupied territories impatient and led to renewed violence. Chiefly responsible for this new wave of terrorism were Islamist (strict Islamic) groups such as Hamas and Islamic Jihad. These groups were popular—and radical—alternatives to the secular, or nonreligious, PLO.

THE OSLO ACCORDS In mid-1992, a
series of secret, informal talks began in Oslo, Norway, between two Israeli academics and a PLO delegation.

Yitzhak Rabin (left) shakes hands with Yasser Arafat at the signing ceremony of the Oslo Accords at the White House, Washington D.C., in September 1993. U.S. president Bill Clinton looks on.

PALESTINIANS AND ISRAELIS KILLED IN ISRAEL AND THE OCCUPIED TERRITORIES, SEPTEMBER 14, 1993–SEPTEMBER 28, 2000

Year	Palestinians killed by Israeli security forces	Palestinians killed by Israeli civilians	Israeli civilians killed by Palestinians	Israeli security forces personnel killed by Palestinians
1993	165	15	36	25
1994	113	39	58	16
1995	423	16	30	
1996	695	41	34	
1997	183	29	0	
1998	217	93		
1999	9 0	22		
2000	140	21		
TOTAL	**451**	**72**	**193**	**111**

(Source: www.btselem.org/English/Statistics/Total_Casualties.asp)

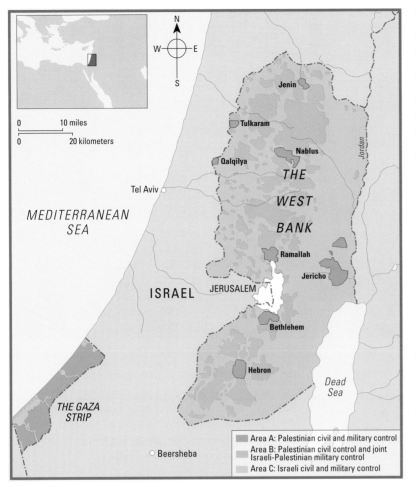

Above: The new distribution of territory as agreed in the Oslo Accords. Under this interim agreement, the West Bank was divided into three areas: Area A was placed under full Palestinian control; Area B was placed under joint Palestinian-Israeli control; and Area C remained under full Israeli control.

Following the signing of the Gaza-Jericho agreement in May 1994, Israeli troops hand over control of their Gaza City base to the Palestinian Authority.

The talks had no official status, although they were conducted with the knowledge and approval of Yossi Beilin, Israel's deputy prime minister. During these talks, the PLO delegation adopted a surprisingly flexible position, in contrast to their attitude at the official talks in Washington, D.C. This attitude, as well as Rabin's realization that the real terrorist threat was now coming from the militant Islamic groups and not the PLO, persuaded him to reverse Israel's refusal to negotiate with the PLO. Soon the Israeli delegation was upgraded to include senior government officials.

Together, the delegates worked out a "Declaration of Principles," which has become the foundation for peace negotiations between Israel and the Palestinians ever since. The Declaration of Principles stated that Israel and the PLO recognized each other's legitimacy, and that Israel would start to withdraw from the occupied territories, beginning with the Gaza Strip and Jericho, over a five-year period. A Palestinian Authority (PA) was formed from the PLO with limited powers of self-rule in the occupied territories.

The document resulting from these talks, known as the Oslo Accords, was signed on September 13, 1993, at a ceremony in Washington, D.C., hosted by U.S. president Bill Clinton. During the ceremony, Yasser Arafat, leader of the PLO, and Yitzhak Rabin, Israeli prime minister, shook hands.

In May 1994, Israel and the PLO signed the Gaza-Jericho agreement in Cairo, Egypt, which led to the establishment of the PA. That month, Israeli forces withdrew from Jericho and most of the Gaza Strip. In November, Rabin handed new powers to the PA, which included responsibility for taxation, health, transportation, and social services. The following October, Israeli forces began a phased withdrawal

from most of the West Bank. In January 1996, Yasser Arafat was elected president of the PA.

THE PEACE PROCESS STALLS

Despite these positive developments, not everyone welcomed the peace process. Militant Palestinian groups such as Hamas were not prepared to recognize Israel under any circumstances, and many ordinary Palestinians were worried that the Oslo Accords did not guarantee the eventual establishment of a Palestinian nation. On the Israeli side, many were concerned that the lands they had fought for would be returned to the Palestinians with no real promise of security in return.

The carrying out of the Oslo Accords took place against a background of increasing terrorist violence toward Israel from Hamas, Islamic Jihad, and a Lebanese-based Shi'ite group called Hezbollah. As more Israelis were killed, popular opinion shifted toward a more hardline approach. Yitzhak Rabin was assassinated in November 1995 by an Israeli extremist opposed to the peace process. In May 1996, a conservative government came to power in Israel, headed by Benjamin Netanyahu, an opponent of the Oslo Accords. Netanyahu claimed to support the peace process, but his government agreed to the expansion

The funeral of Yitzhak Rabin. Although the Israeli prime minister was a joint winner of the 1994 Nobel Peace Prize for his efforts in promoting peace with the Palestinians, he was also hated by right-wing Israelis who blamed him for giving away too much.

of Israeli settlements in the occupied territories, which went against the spirit of the agreement.

The United States put pressure on the Israelis to put a stop to settlement building and to continue with the troop withdrawals. In October 1998, Netanyahu and Arafat signed a new agreement in Washington, D.C., known as the Wye Memorandum. Israel agreed to withdraw from an additional 13 per cent of the West Bank in return for a pledge from the Palestinians to crack down on terrorism.

CAMP DAVID II In July 2000, U.S. president Clinton invited the new Israeli prime minister, Ehud Barak, and Yasser Arafat to Camp David to negotiate the final status of the occupied territories and Jerusalem. By this time, Israeli withdrawals had left 40 percent of the West Bank and 65 percent of the Gaza Strip under the full or partial control of the PA. Barak insisted that East Jerusalem, plus 80 percent of the land containing the Jewish settlements on the West Bank, would remain part of Israel. The rest could be

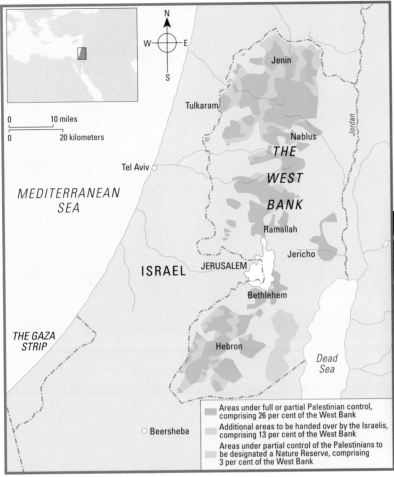

handed over to the PA. Barak's proposal was more than any Israeli leader had previously offered, but Arafat insisted that Israel withdraw from the vast majority of the occupied territories, including East Jerusalem. Although Barak was being criticized in Israel for having offered too much, no agreement could be reached.

Areas under full or partial Palestinian control, comprising 26 per cent of the West Bank

Additional areas to be handed over by the Israelis, comprising 13 per cent of the West Bank

Areas under partial control of the Palestinians to be designated a Nature Reserve, comprising 3 per cent of the West Bank

A map showing the agreed reallocations of territory under the Wye Memorandum of November 1998. An additional 12 percent of the West Bank would be transferred from Area C to Area B, and 1 percent would move from Area C to Area A.

Israeli prime minister Netanyahu (left) and Yasser Arafat meet with President Clinton at the White House on October 15, 1998. The Wye Memorandum was signed eight days later.

ISRAELI SETTLER POPULATION GROWTH IN THE WEST BANK AND GAZA STRIP, 1972–2001

Year	West Bank (not including East Jerusalem)	Gaza Strip	Total
1972	800	700	1,500
1983	22,800	900	23,700
1989	69,800	3,000	72,800
1992	101,100	4,300	105,400
1995	133,200	5,300	138,500
1998	161,300	6,100	167,400
2001	201,800	6,500	208,300

(Source: www.fmep.org/images/charts/chart00074.jpg)

CHAPTER 7
THE SECOND INTIFADA AND THE ROAD MAP

A Palestinian rioter hurls stones at a tank in a West Bank town during the second intifada, or popular rising.

The frustration felt by many Palestinians about the slow progress of the peace process, combined with continuing social and economic hardship, led to renewed violence in the occupied territories in late 2000. The spark for this second intifada came on September 28, 2000, when Ariel Sharon, leader of Likud, Israel's most powerful right-wing party, visited Temple Mount in Jerusalem. Temple Mount is the site of al-Aqsa mosque, a holy Muslim shrine, as well as the Biblical First and Second Temples, which are sacred to Jews and important to Christians.

Sharon was accompanied by party colleagues and about 1,000 armed riot police, and his visit resulted in widespread protests among Palestinians in Jerusalem. During these demonstrations, Israeli police shot and killed six unarmed protesters. Outrage at these killings led to over a month of rioting in the West Bank and Gaza Strip.

This second intifada was led by Islamists and local leaders of Fatah, the largest and most radical faction of the PLO. The leaders demanded total Israeli withdrawal from the occupied territories, the removal of all Jewish settlements,

the establishment of a sovereign nation of Palestine with its capital in Jerusalem, and the right of return of all Palestinian refugees. They criticized PLO leader Yasser Arafat for offering the Israelis too much in peace negotiations and faulted the PA for providing weak leadership and poor services.

A rise in suicide bombings and other terrorist attacks inside Israel accompanied the second intifada. By April 2002, this terrorism had caused over 160 civilian deaths. The organizations that carried out the attacks—Hamas, Islamic Jihad, and the al-Aqsa Martyrs Brigade, a militant wing of Fatah—had an especially extreme goal: the complete destruction of Israel.

Israel called upon the PA to crack down on the rioters and terrorists, and the PA security forces did occasionally carry out mass arrests of Islamists and members of terrorist groups. The violence continued, however, so in 2001 Israel sent its own armed forces into the occupied territories to attack the rioters and terrorist bases directly.

In December 2001, Yasser Arafat also became a target of Israeli anger. The Israelis claimed he had not cracked down on the terrorists and had even given them his unspoken support. For the next five months, Arafat became a virtual prisoner as Israeli tanks surrounded his compound in the West Bank town of Ramallah. The action against Arafat, however, resulted in increased support for him among Palestinian militants.

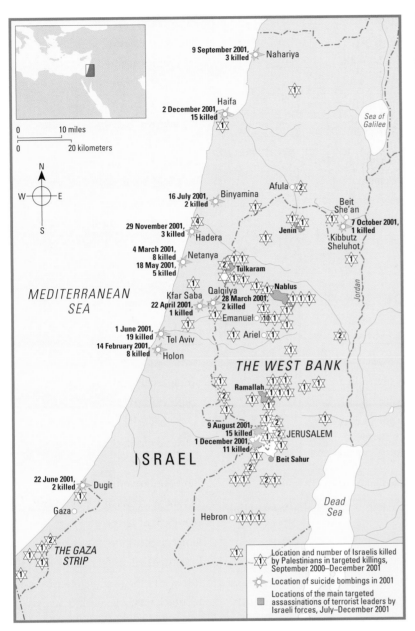

9 September 2001,
3 killed — Nahariya

Haifa
2 December 2001,
15 killed

Sea of
Galilee

Afula

16 July 2001,
2 killed — Binyamina

Beit
She'an

7 October 2001,
1 killed

29 November 2001,
3 killed — Hadera

Jenin

Kibbutz
Sheluhot

4 March 2001,
8 killed
18 May 2001,
5 killed — Netanya

Tulkaram

MEDITERRANEAN
SEA

Kfar Saba
22 April 2001,
1 killed

Qalqilya
28 March 2001,
2 killed — Nablus

Emanuel

1 June 2001,
19 killed — Tel Aviv
14 February 2001,
8 killed — Holon

Ariel

Jordan

THE WEST BANK

Ramallah

9 August 2001,
15 killed
1 December 2001,
11 killed — JERUSALEM

Beit Sahur

ISRAEL

22 June 2001,
2 killed — Dugit

Gaza

Hebron

Dead
Sea

THE GAZA
STRIP

Location and number of Israelis killed
by Palestinians in targeted killings,
September 2000–December 2001

Location of suicide bombings in 2001

Locations of the main targeted
assassinations of terrorist leaders by
Israeli forces, July–December 2001

Above: Bombs carried by two
suicide bombers explode in
Jerusalem on December 1, 2001,
killing at least eight people.

Left: Terrorist attacks on
Israelis and the assassinations
of terrorist leaders by Israeli
forces during 2000 and 2001.
As attacks on troops and civilians
mounted, the Israelis began to
target people who were directing
the violence.

THE SECOND INTIFADA

(Figures apply to the period September 29, 2000–June 1, 2003)

Year	Palestinians killed by Israeli security forces	Palestinians killed by Israeli civilians	Israeli civilians killed by Palestinians	Israeli security forces personnel killed by Palestinians
2000	272	6	18	19
2001	454	7	65	21
2002	990	13	88	101
2003 (to June 1)	305	6	16	18
TOTAL	**2,021**	**32**	**187**	**159**

(Source: www.btselem.org/English/Statistics/TotalCasualties.asp)

Between April and June 2002, in response to a wave of suicide bombings, Israeli forces invaded and reoccupied the West Bank towns of Ramallah, Bethlehem, Jenin, Tulkaram, Qalqilya, Nablus and Hebron. PA buildings and suspected terrorist bases were shelled, weapons were confiscated, house-to-house searches were conducted, arrests were made, and strict curfews were imposed. The Palestinians claimed the Israelis massacred civilians in Jenin. Israel insisted it had merely responded to organized armed resistance. The UN Security Council demanded that Israel withdraw from the reoccupied West Bank towns without delay.

THE "ROAD MAP TO PEACE" In April 2003, a new peace plan was announced. Known as the "road map to peace," it was drawn up by the UN, the United States, the European Union, and Russia, with Israeli and Palestinian consultation. The plan sought

Right: Water resources on the West Bank. Access to water supplies for Palestinians and Israelis remains an important issue that will need to be resolved before a lasting peace can be achieved.

An Israeli tank, searching for Palestinian militants, blocks access to a refugee camp in Jenin, June 2002.

An Israeli soldier passes a sign protesting the building of the security fence through a Palestinian village on the West Bank.

a solution to the conflict by creating an independent Palestinian nation in the occupied territories that would exist alongside Israel. This plan set out to achieve its goal—in three stages—by 2005.

The first stage required the following: the end of Palestinian violence; the reform of Palestinian political institutions (which had been accused of corruption and tacit support of terrorism); the dismantling of all Israeli settlements in the occupied territories established since March 2001; and progressive Israeli withdrawal from designated areas of the occupied territories. Stage two would involve the creation of an independent Palestinian nation. There would also be discussions at this stage on crucial issues such as the sharing of water resources and economic development. At stage three, the parties would reach agreement on final borders, the status of Jerusalem, the return of Palestinian refugees, and Israeli settlements—all of which would lead to a permanent end to the conflict.

Before the plan's publication, Yasser Arafat came under increasing pressure to step down as leader of the PA. Although Arafat remained popular with Palestinians, his failure to clamp down on terrorism had discredited him in the eyes of many in the international community. In March 2003, Arafat appointed Mahmoud Abbas the prime minister of the PA. Abbas was a strong believer in the peace process, and Arafat surrendered many of his powers to him.

There was progress on the plan in June 2003, when a cease-fire was declared by the terrorist groups, and Israel began to withdraw its forces from the occupied territories and release some Palestinian prisoners. Any optimism quickly faded, however, when terrorist attacks were renewed in August, and Israeli troops halted their withdrawals and began to assassinate top terrorist leaders. On September 6, Mahmoud Abbas resigned after emerging the loser in a power struggle

An 8-mile (13-km) stretch of the security fence will be in the form of a concrete wall (above) that will be built around the town of Qalqilya and will separate parts of Jerusalem from adjacent Palestinian areas.

with Arafat and having failed to control Palestinian violence. Arafat appointed Ahmed Qureia as his replacement. As suicide bombings continued, Israel vowed to exile—or possibly assassinate—Yasser Arafat.

THE FUTURE While the international community continues to promote peace in the region, recent developments are making the road map—or any similar effort that seeks a solution to the conflict by creating a separate Palestinian nation—more and more unlikely. Since April 2003, Israel has begun constructing a "security fence" around the Palestinian-controlled territories as a means of protecting itself and ending terrorist attacks. There are fears that the 20-foot (6-m) high fence, which is topped with barbed wire and lined with guard towers, will make it very difficult to establish a workable, independent Palestinian nation, because the fence blocks access to

the resources the nation would need to function and thrive.

On the Israeli side of the fence, new houses are being built for Jewish settlements in the West Bank. New roads, electricity and water supplies, and communication lines are binding these settlements ever more closely to the Israeli nation. Israelis increasingly see these settlements as permanent parts of their country that cannot be given away during peace talks.

New homes being built at the Jewish West Bank settlement of Ariel in June 2003, despite international pressure on Israel to stop expanding its settlements.

Increasing numbers of Palestinians now despair of ever achieving an independent nation of Palestine. They are starting to believe that their only choice is to accept Israel's control of their land and to demand equal rights.

This one-nation solution might not be welcomed by Jewish Israelis, because within a few years, such a nation could lose its Jewish majority. There are currently 5.4 million Jews and 4.93 million Arabs in Israel and the occupied territories. It is estimated that by 2020—due to the higher birth rate of Arabs compared to Jews—there will be 6.69 million Jews and 8.49 million Arabs. With Arabs demanding equal rights and "one citizen, one vote," there may well be pressure on Israel to abandon its Jewish identity. Israel's Jewish community would of course stubbornly resist any such move.

The current state of the Arab-Israeli conflict is marked by periodic moves toward peace followed by sudden outbreaks of

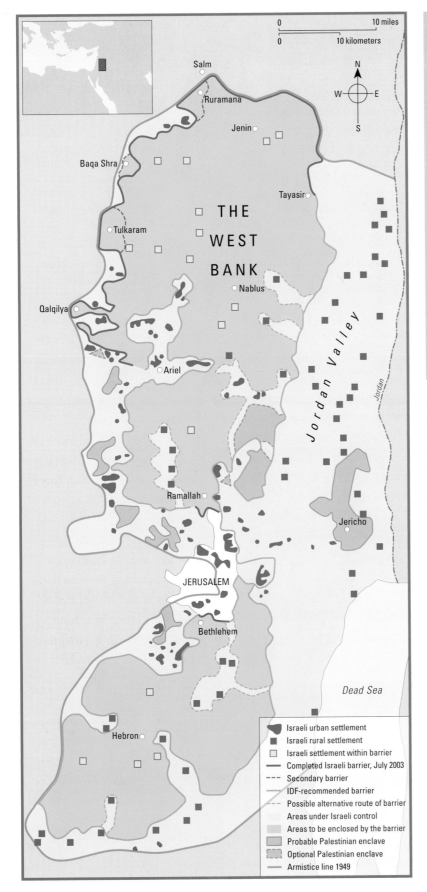

THE WEST BANK

Salm
Ruramana
Jenin
Baqa Shra
Tayasir
Tulkaram
Nablus
Qalqilya
Ariel
Jordan Valley
Ramallah
Jericho
JERUSALEM
Bethlehem
Dead Sea
Hebron

■ Israeli urban settlement
■ Israeli rural settlement
□ Israeli settlement within barrier
— Completed Israeli barrier, July 2003
--- Secondary barrier
— IDF-recommended barrier
--- Possible alternative route of barrier
Areas under Israeli control
Areas to be enclosed by the barrier
Probable Palestinian enclave
Optional Palestinian enclave
— Armistice line 1949

0   10 miles
0   10 kilometers

FEAR OF WAR

"As one who participated in all the wars of the state of Israel, I saw the horror of wars. I saw the fear of wars. I saw my best friends being killed in battles. I was seriously injured twice . . . I believe I understand the importance of peace, not more but not less than many of the politicians who speak about peace, but never had this experience."

—Israeli prime minister Ariel Sharon, July 2003

A map showing the projected route of the security fence in the West Bank. In October 2003, the UN passed a resolution stating the barrier was "in contradiction to international law." Israeli public opinion, however, is strongly in favor of the fence.

renewed violence, and there seems little prospect of an immediate resolution. The Middle East has seen some surprising examples of progress toward peace, however, such as the treaties between Israel and Egypt in 1979 and Israel and Jordan in 1994. There is always a chance—through pressure from the international community and enlightened leadership—that the parties currently locked in battle might discover a way of sharing the land and resources over which they are now fighting. If so, they may bring to an end a conflict that began over a century ago.

ABBAS, MAHMOUD (1935–)
Also known as Abu Mazen, Abbas was born in Safad, Palestine. He was a founding member of Fatah and has been a member of the PLO Executive Committee since 1968. He has headed the PLO Department for National and International Relations since 1980. Abbas is considered a moderate and is strongly in favor of a peaceful settlement with Israel. He coordinated negotiations during the Madrid conference and the Oslo Accords. Although popular in the international community, Abbas lacks support among ordinary Palestinians. He was prime minister of the PA for just four months, in 2003, before he was replaced.

ALLON, YIGAL (1918–1980)
An Israeli military commander and politician, Allon was born in Galilee. He was a cofounder in 1941 of the Palmah, a highly trained Zionist commando unit, becoming its commander in 1945. During the 1947–1949 War, he commanded the southern front, driving invading Arab armies from Israel. In 1954, he was elected to the Knesset, and from 1961 to 1968 he served as Minister of Labor. He became deputy prime minister in 1968 and then Minister of Education and Culture. From 1974 to 1977, he was Foreign Minister.

ARAFAT, YASSER (1929–)
The leader of the PLO was born in Gaza. In 1958, he met fellow Palestinian activist Abu Jihad. He then moved to Jerusalem, where he founded Fatah in 1959. Arafat was elected chairman of the PLO in 1969. After the PLO's clash with Jordan in 1971, he moved to Lebanon. He remained there until besieged by the Israeli army in 1982, after which he moved to Tunisia. During the 1970s and 1980s, Arafat gradually changed the PLO from a terrorist group into an organization resembling a government-in-exile, committed to seeking a peaceful settlement with Israel. In 1993, he signed the Oslo Accords with Israel. He returned to the occupied territories in 1994, and in 1996 he was elected president of the PA. Since then, he has increasingly been seen by Israel and the United States as an obstacle to peace because of his refusal to condemn Palestinian militants. He was placed under house arrest between December 2001 and April 2002, and in 2003 the Israeli government threatened him with permanent exile. Yet he remains a popular figure among Palestinians.

ASAD, HAFIZ (1930–2000)
Asad was born at Qardaha in Syria. In 1964, he entered the Syrian government and rose to become leader of a faction of the ruling Ba'ath Party. That faction seized power in 1970, and Asad became president of Syria, a post he held until his death.

ASHWARI, HANAN (1946–)
A Palestinian academic and politician, Ashwari became the official spokeswoman for the Palestinian delegation during the peace conferences of 1991 to 1993. She promoted a moderate and reasonable image of the Palestinian cause to the rest of the world. Ashwari was elected as an independent to the Palestinian Legislative Council in 1996.

BAKER, JAMES (1930–)
As U.S. secretary of state from 1989 to 1992, Baker worked hard at promoting a peaceful settlement to the Arab-Israeli conflict. In March 1991, he became the first U.S. secretary of state to meet with a Palestinian delegation. His attempts at setting up a general Middle East peace conference were impeded by Israel's insistence that it would only conduct bilateral talks with individual Arab countries.

BALFOUR, ARTHUR JAMES (1848–1930)
As British foreign secretary from 1916 to 1919, Balfour proclaimed British support for establishing a Jewish nation in Palestine in the famous Balfour Declaration of 1917. Balfour had previously served as prime minister from 1902 to 1905.

BARAK, EHUD (1942–)
Born in Kibbutz Mishmar Hasharon, Barak joined the Israeli Defense Force in 1959 and served in various positions of command in the 1967, 1973, and 1982 wars. In April 1991, he was appointed chief of the general staff and was promoted to lieutenant general, the highest rank in the Israeli military. Barak oversaw the IDF's redeployment in Gaza and Jericho following the May 1994 agreement, and he played a major role in the peace treaty with Jordan. Elected as a member of the Labor Party to the Knesset in 1996, he served as prime minister and minister of defense from May 1999 to February 2001.

BEGIN, MENACHEM (1913–1992)
A passionate Zionist from an early age, Begin was born in Brest-Litovsk (in present-day Belarus). In the 1930s, he lived in eastern Europe, where he fought on behalf of Jews and arranged for their immigration to Palestine. In the

1940s, he joined the Jewish terrorist organization Irgun, organizing various attacks on the British. Beginning in 1948, Begin was a right-wing opposition party leader in the Knesset, and in 1977 he was elected prime minister. He helped initiate the peace process with Egypt that led to the 1979 Israel-Egypt Peace Treaty. Begin's government launched Operation Peace for Galilee, Israel's invasion of Lebanon in 1982.

BEN-GURION, DAVID
(1886–1973)
Israel's first prime minister, Ben-Gurion was born in Plonsk, Poland, and was a leader of a Zionist youth group in his teens. He moved to Palestine in 1906 and helped set up the first kibbutz (an agricultural workers' commune). In 1935, he was elected chairman of the World Zionist Organization, and he was a leader in the struggle to establish the nation of Israel. In May 1948, he became prime minister and defense minister of the new state, and he oversaw the establishment of Israel's institutions, the development of new towns, and the settlement of outlying areas. He also led Israel during the 1956 Suez War, finally resigning as prime minister in 1963.

BUSH, GEORGE HERBERT WALKER (1924–)
As president of the United States from 1989 to 1993, George Bush organized a coalition of Western and Arab nations that combined to defeat Saddam Hussein's Iraq in the 1991 Gulf War. Out of gratitude for Arab support in the Gulf War, Bush placed pressure on Israel to participate in a general Middle East peace conference.

BUSH, GEORGE WALKER (1946–)
The 43rd president of the United States, Bush was elected in 2000. Following the September 11, 2001 terrorist attacks, Bush declared war

on terrorism. Islamist terror groups such as Al Qaeda, Hezbollah, and Hamas—and the countries that supported them—became targets in this new kind of war. In April 2003, Bush put his influence behind a new attempt to end the Arab-Israeli conflict, authorizing the creation of the "road map to peace."

CARTER, JIMMY (1924–)
As U.S. president from 1977 to 1981, Carter was instrumental in mediating the Egypt-Israel Peace Treaty of 1979. He was a committed supporter of Israel but believed the Palestinians should have a homeland and be compensated for the losses they had suffered. He invited Israeli prime minister Begin and Egyptian president Sadat to the presidential retreat at Camp David for a conference that lasted from September 4–17, 1978, a meeting that led to the peace treaty signed the following year.

CLINTON, BILL (1946-)
As U.S. president from 1993 to 2001, Bill Clinton worked tirelessly to promote peace in the Middle East. In 1993, he hosted the signing of the Declaration of Principles on the White House lawn. The Clinton administration encouraged bilateral talks between Israel and Jordan that led to the signing of the July 1994 Washington Declaration. Clinton led a new diplomatic push for peace in 1998, leading to the Wye Memorandum, signed by Israeli prime minister Netanyahu and Arafat in October. In July 2000, Clinton hosted a Camp David Peace Summit between Israeli prime minister Barak and Arafat, which ended without agreement.

DAYAN, MOSHE (1915–1981)
Born in Galilee, Dayan was just 14 when he joined the Haganah, a Jewish underground organization that defended Jewish settlements from Arab attacks. In 1941, he joined the British army in the

Middle East and lost his left eye during a battle in Lebanon. During the 1947–1949 war, Dayan led the defense of Jewish settlements in the Jordan Valley and helped to defeat Egyptian forces in the south. In the 1950s, he organized raids on Arab positions in Gaza and elsewhere and led Israel's Suez campaign in 1956. In 1959, he entered the Knesset. He served as minister of agriculture from 1959 to 1964 and then as Minister of Defense from 1967 to 1974. It was Dayan who persuaded the Israeli government to launch the preemptive strike that began the Six-Day War and to attack the Golan Heights. He was criticized after Egypt's surprise attack in 1973, which led to his resignation. As foreign minister between 1977 and 1979, Dayan was instrumental in negotiating the Camp David Accords with Egypt.

EBAN, ABBA (1915–2002)
An Israeli diplomat and politician, as foreign minister Eban worked to maintain Israel's good relations with the United States and to establish an association with the European community. During the 1960s, Eban fought for Israel's cause at the United Nations.

ESHKOL, LEVI (1895–1969)
Born in Oratovo in the Ukraine, Eshkol joined a Zionist group as a youth and came to Palestine at 19. In 1940, he joined the Haganah, and in 1947 he helped to establish the Israeli Defense Force. He was a minister of agriculture and of finance, obtaining funds to develop the country and equip the army, and he become prime minister in 1963. He died in office. He is widely credited with providing the IDF with the funding and equipment necessary to win the 1967 war.

HERZL, THEODOR
(1860–1904)
The founder of the Zionist movement was born in Budapest,

Hungary. As a student in Vienna and later as a journalist in Paris, he was appalled by the anti-Semitism he encountered. Herzl believed that anti-Semitism would always be a factor in society, and the only solution for Jews was their mass emigration to a land they could call their own. In 1896, he published *The Jewish State*, in which he expanded on this idea. Herzl formed the Zionist Organization and collected funds from Jews around the world to help realize his dream. In 1897, the First Zionist Congress was held at Basle, Switzerland. By the time of Herzl's death, Zionism had become a mass movement. His remains were brought to Israel in 1949 and reinterred on Mount Herzl in Jerusalem.

HUSSEIN, KING OF JORDAN (1935–1999)

Born in Amman, King Hussein bin Talal assumed the throne of Jordan in 1952. Throughout his 47-year-reign, he struggled to promote peace in the Middle East. After the 1967 war, he helped draft UN Resolution 242 calling on Israel to withdraw from the occupied territories in exchange for peace. In 1991, he played an important role in bringing about the Madrid Peace Conference, providing the means for Palestinians to negotiate their future and also negotiating Jordan's own peace treaty with Israel.

HUSSEIN, SADDAM (1937–)

The ruthless Iraqi dictator came to power in 1979 with ambitions to make Iraq a regional superpower. In 1980, he invaded Iran, beginning an eight-year war that ended in stalemate, and in 1990 he invaded Kuwait. A U.S.-led coalition defeated Iraq and forced its retreat from Kuwait in the 1991 Gulf War. His regime was overthrown by coalition forces in the second Gulf War in 2003, and Hussein fled to an unknown destination. In

December 2003, he was captured by U.S. Special Forces and held in custody pending his future trial.

JIHAD, ABU (1935–1988)

Cofounder, with Yasser Arafat, of Fatah in 1959, Jihad became the military chief of Fatah in the 1960s. He established PLO relations with Jordan, Syria, and Saudi Arabia, and he organized the Palestinian resistance in the occupied territories. A close ally of Arafat, Jihad was appointed his official deputy in 1980. Israeli agents assassinated Jihad in 1988.

KISSINGER, HENRY (1923–)

As secretary of state under U.S. presidents Nixon and Ford, Kissinger guided U.S. foreign policy from 1969 to 1975. He played an important role in negotiating a cease-fire in the Middle East after the 1973 war, and he won the 1973 Nobel Peace Prize.

MEIR, GOLDA (1898–1978)

Born in Russia and educated in the United States, Meir emigrated to Palestine in 1921. She was active in the struggle against the British and served in various government ministries after 1948. In 1965, she helped to form the Israel Labour Party. She became prime minister in 1969. Meir accepted blame for Israel's lack of preparation in the 1973 war and resigned in 1974.

MUBARAK, MUHAMMAD HOSNI (1928–)

The president of Egypt since 1981, Mubarak began his career in the Egyptian air force. In 1975, he was appointed vice president. He assumed the presidency after Anwar Sadat's assassination. Mubarak oversaw the handing back of the last third of the Sinai in April 1982 and has sought to maintain peaceful relations with Israel. He aligned Egypt with the coalition forces in the 1991 Gulf War and has dealt harshly with

Islamist opposition groups in Egypt, leading to an attempt on his life in 1995.

NASSER, GAMAL ABDEL (1918–1970)

The Egyptian president came to power as leader of a revolutionary group from within the Egyptian army called the Free Officers, who overthrew the king in 1952. Nasser was officially elected president in 1956. Nasser hoped to modernize Egypt by building the Aswan Dam, which would allow more of Egypt's land to be farmed, produce electricity, and allow water to be stored for times of drought. After the United States cancelled a loan for the dam, he nationalized the Suez Canal in hopes of using it to raise funds. The Suez War of 1956 made Nasser a hero in the Arab world. He formed the United Arab Republic with Syria in 1958, but the union was dissolved in 1961 after a coup in Syria. After Egypt's defeat in the 1967 Six-Day War, Nasser resigned, but the people took to the streets and demanded his return to government.

NETANYAHU, BENJAMIN (1949–)

Born in Tel Aviv and educated in the United States, Netanyahu returned to Israel in 1967 and enlisted in the IDF, serving in an elite anti-terror unit and achieving the rank of captain. Since 1979, he has organized conferences and written books on countering international terrorism. He served as Israeli ambassador to the UN during the 1980s. In 1988, Netanyahu was elected to the Knesset as a Likud member and was appointed deputy foreign minister. In 1993, he became Likud Party Chairman and served as Israeli prime minister from 1996 to 1999, during which time he was accused of hindering the peace process by allowing Jewish settlement building to continue.

PERES, SHIMON (1923–)
Born in Poland, Peres moved to Palestine in 1934, where he joined the Haganah in 1947. From 1953 to 1959, he served as director general of the defense ministry, developing Israel's aircraft industry and nuclear program. In 1959, he was elected to the Knesset, and he has remained a member ever since, serving in various ministries. He was Israeli prime minister from 1984 to 1986 and from 1995 to 1996. During the 1990s, Peres worked hard to maintain the momentum of the peace process and shared the Nobel Peace Prize in 1994.

RABIN, YITZHAK
(1922–1995)
Rabin was born in Jerusalem and served in the Palmach (Jewish commando unit) and then the Israeli Defense Force for 27 years. After retiring from the military in 1968, he was appointed Israeli ambassador to the United States. In 1973, he was elected to the Knesset, and he served as prime minister from 1974 to 1977. He focused on improving the economy and strengthening the IDF, and in 1975 he concluded the interim peace agreement with Egypt. Rabin was elected prime minister again in 1992, and he made the decision to negotiate directly with the PLO. In 1993, he and Yasser Arafat signed the Declaration of Principles in Washington, D.C. The following year, he signed the Gaza-Jericho Agreement and the Israel-Jordan peace treaty and shared the Nobel Peace Prize. On November 4, 1995, Rabin was assassinated by a Jewish extremist in Tel Aviv.

REAGAN, RONALD (1911–)
As U.S. president from 1981 to 1989, Reagan was a strong supporter of Israel and believed in maintaining Israeli military superiority in the Middle East. Under his presidency, the United States initiated various Middle East peace plans, including the Reagan Plan and the Schultz Plan (which is named after U.S. secretary of state George Schultz).

SADAT, ANWAR (1918–1981)
Beginning in 1952, Sadat served as Nasser's public relations minister and trusted deputy, but he was fairly unknown when he became president of Egypt in 1970. He quickly proved a bold and decisive leader, offering Israel a peace treaty in return for the Sinai lands and expelling Soviet advisors when the Soviet Union proved an unreliable ally. He also secretly planned a surprise attack on Israel to retake the Sinai after his peace initiatives were rebuffed, and the attack was carried out in October 1973. Egyptian forces were soon repelled, but Sadat's move had created a new momentum for a peace settlement, which he accelerated with a visit to Israel in 1977. This visit led to the Camp David Accords and the eventual peace treaty with Israel in 1979. Sadat won the Nobel Peace Prize for his efforts, but his recognition of Israel aroused popular anger among Islamists at home, and he was assassinated by Muslim fundamentalists in 1981.

SHAMIR, YITZHAK (1915–)
Born in Poland, Shamir came to Palestine in 1935 and joined the Jewish terrorist organization Irgun, directed against the British occupation, and later the Stern Gang, a militant faction of Irgun. After Israeli independence, Shamir joined Mossad, Israel's intelligence service, and he was elected to the Knesset in 1973 as a member for Likud. He became foreign minister in 1980 and was prime minister from 1983 to 1984. A hard-liner, Shamir opposed Israel's peace treaty with Egypt and the withdrawal from Lebanon. He softened his stance when he returned to office in 1990, agreeing not to respond to Iraq's Scud missile strikes and taking part in the Madrid peace talks. He stepped down from the Likud leadership in 1993.

SHARON, ARIEL (1928–)
Born in Kfar Malal, Sharon joined the Haganah at age 14 and commanded an infantry company in the 1947–1949 war. In 1953, he led the "101" special commando unit that carried out border raids, and he commanded a paratroop corps in the 1956 war. In the 1967 and 1973 wars, he was commander of an armored division, and in the latter conflict he led the crossing of the Suez Canal, which brought victory. He was elected to the Knesset in 1973 and again in 1977, serving as agriculture and defense ministers. He organized the 1982 invasion of Lebanon but resigned when he was found indirectly responsible for massacres at the Sabra and Shatila refugee camps in west Beirut. He continued in government, serving in various ministries, before becoming Likud party leader in 1999. He became prime minister in 2001 and was reelected in 2003.

WEIZMANN, CHAIM
(1874–1952)
Born in Russia, Weizman became active in the Zionist movement while studying in Europe. His scientific assistance to the Allies during World War I brought him into close contact with British leaders, giving him crucial influence over British policy toward Palestine—the issuing of the Balfour Declaration in 1917 is partly attributed to Weizmann. In 1920, he became president of the World Zionist Organization. He played a key role in the adoption of the partition plan by the UN in 1947 and in the United States' recognition of Israel. Weizmann served as the first president of Israel from 1948 until his death four years later.

TIME LINE

1890s
Beginning of Zionist movement.

1900s
Clashes between Palestinian Arabs and Jewish settlers.

1917
Balfour Declaration.

1921
Start of British Mandate.

NOVEMBER 29, 1947
UN General Assembly votes to accept Palestine partition plan.

DECEMBER 1947
War between Palestinian Arabs and Jews begins.

APRIL 1, 1948
Zionist offensive begins.

MAY 15, 1948
British Mandate ends. Zionist leaders declare the founding of the nation of Israel.

MAY 16–17, 1948
Arab nations invade Israel.

JUNE 11–JULY 8, 1948
UN-negotiated cease-fire.

JULY 8–18, 1948
Israeli offensives capture many new towns, enlarging Israeli territory.

JULY 18–OCTOBER 15, 1948
UN-negotiated cease-fire. Israel establishes itself in newly conquered territory.

1948–1949
725,000 Palestinian Arabs become refugees.

FEBRUARY–JULY 1949
Armistice agreements signed by Israel and the Arab nations.

JULY 1956
Nasser nationalizes the Suez Canal.

OCTOBER 29, 1956
Israeli forces invade Gaza Strip and the Sinai Peninsula.

OCTOBER 31, 1956
British and French forces launch joint attack on Egypt.

NOVEMBER 5, 1956
Under U.S. pressure, Britain and France agree to cease-fire.

DECEMBER 22, 1956
Anglo-French troops are evacuated.

MARCH 1957
Israel withdraws from the Sinai Peninsula and Gaza Strip.

AUGUST 1963
Israel begins implementing its National Water Carrier Plan, leading to a near-conflict with Syria.

1964
Formation of PLO.

APRIL–MAY 1967
Border clashes between Israel and Syria.

MAY 18, 1967
Nasser demands the withdrawal of UN peacekeeping forces in the Sinai Peninsula.

MAY 21, 1967
Nasser closes the Straits of Tiran.

MAY 30, 1967
Egypt and Jordan sign a mutual defense treaty.

JUNE 5, 1967
Israel launches an air attack on Egypt's airfields that virtually destroys the Egyptian air force on the ground and follows with a ground invasion of Gaza and the Sinai. Jordanian and Syrian armies begin shelling Israeli positions. Israel destroys Jordan's air force and most of Syria's air force.

JUNE 6, 1967
Israel captures Ramallah and Jenin.

JUNE 7, 1967
Israel captures East Jerusalem and Nablus.

JUNE 8, 1967
Israel completes its reconquest of Gaza, the Sinai, and the West Bank.

JUNE 9, 1967
Israel launches an invasion of Golan Heights.

JUNE 10, 1967
Israel completes conquest of Golan Heights. Cease-fire agreed.

NOVEMBER 1967
UN Resolution 242 calls upon Israel to withdraw from territories seized in June.

1970–1971
PLO is driven from Jordan and forced into southern Lebanon.

FEBRUARY 1971
Egyptian leader Sadat offers peace with Israel in return for Israeli withdrawal from the Sinai.

OCTOBER 6, 1973
Egypt and Syria launch joint invasion of Israel.

OCTOBER 11, 1973
Syrian forces are pushed back to their own frontier.

OCTOBER 16–17, 1973
Israeli forces cross Suez Canal,

cutting off supplies to Egyptian armies in the Sinai Peninsula.

OCTOBER 20, 1973
Egypt and Israel agree to cease-fire.

OCTOBER 22, 1973
Syria and Israel agree to cease-fire.

MARCH 5, 1974
Israeli forces withdraw from west bank of Suez Canal.

MAY 31, 1974
UN peacekeeping force are established in Golan Heights.

SEPTEMBER 1975
Israel withdraws most of its troops from the Sinai and a UN-policed buffer zone is established between Egyptian and Israeli forces.

NOVEMBER 1977
Sadat visits Israel in efforts to secure peace.

MARCH 1978
Israel launches Operation Litani, attacking PLO bases in southern Lebanon.

JUNE 1978
Israeli forces withdraw from southern Lebanon.

SEPTEMBER 1978
Israel-Egypt discussions take place at Camp David.

JUNE 6, 1982
Israel launches Operation Peace for Galilee, a full-scale invasion of Lebanon.

JUNE 13, 1982
Siege of Beirut begins.

JUNE 9–10, 1982
Israeli Air Force destroys Syrian missile batteries in Bekaa Valley and defeats Syrian air force.

JUNE 11, 1982
Israel and Syria agree to cease-fire.

AUGUST 12, 1982
Israeli siege of Beirut ends with an agreement on a cease-fire, and arrangements are made for PLO fighters to be evacuated from Lebanon.

OCTOBER 23, 1983
Terrorist bombing kills 241 U.S. Marines stationed in Beirut.

JUNE 1985
Israel withdraws from most of Lebanon, maintaining a 5-mile (8-km) wide security zone along the border.

DECEMBER 8, 1987
Start of the first intifada.

NOVEMBER 1988
PLO recognizes the nation of Israel.

AUGUST 2, 1990
Iraqi forces invade Kuwait.

JANUARY 16, 1991
Gulf War begins

JANUARY–FEBRUARY 1991
Iraq fires 39 Scud missiles at Israel.

FEBRUARY 27, 1991
Gulf War ends. Kuwait is liberated.

OCTOBER 1991
Middle East peace conference held in Madrid.

JULY 1992
Discussions begin in Oslo between Palestinian and Israeli delegations.

SEPTEMBER 13, 1993
Oslo Accords signed in Washington, D.C. End of first intifada.

MAY 1994
Israel and the PLO sign the Gaza-Jericho agreement in Cairo.

OCTOBER 1994
Israeli forces begin phased withdrawal from most of the West Bank.

NOVEMBER 1995
Israeli prime minister Yitzhak Rabin is assassinated.

JANUARY 1996
Yasser Arafat elected president of the PA.

OCTOBER 1998
Wye Memorandum signed in Washington, D.C. by Yasser Arafat and Benjamin Netanyahu.

MAY 2000
Israeli forces withdraw completely from Lebanon.

JULY 2000
Barak and Arafat meet at Camp David for final negotiations on peace plan. Talks end in deadlock.

SEPTEMBER 28, 2000
Second intifada begins when Ariel Sharon visits Temple Mount, sparking widespread protests.

DECEMBER 2001
Israeli tanks surround Arafat's headquarters in Ramallah, keeping him a virtual prisoner.

APRIL–JUNE 2002
Israeli forces invade and reoccupy seven West Bank towns in order to destroy terrorist infrastructure.

MARCH 2003
Mahmoud Abbas appointed Palestinian prime minister.

APRIL 2003
"Road map to peace," a new, internationally backed plan to bring peace to the Middle East by 2005, is announced. Israel begins building its "separation fence" between Palestinian-controlled areas and Jewish settlements on the West Bank.

SEPTEMBER 6, 2003
Abbas resigns as Palestinian prime minister.

activist A person who takes action in pursuit of a political goal.

annex Take over territory and make it part of a nation.

anti-Semitism Hostility toward Jews.

armistice An agreement between the opposing sides in a conflict to stop fighting temporarily, pending peace negotiations.

artillery Large guns or other heavy arms.

autonomy Political independence and self-government.

beachhead A part of an enemy shoreline that troops have captured and are using as a base for launching an attack further inland.

besiege Surround a place such as a city with armed forces in order to bring about its capture or surrender.

bilateral Involving two sides.

blockade The blocking of approaches to an area to prevent people or goods from entering or leaving.

boycott Refuse to take part in an activity or organization or buy certain products or services, as a form of protest.

brigades Large units of an army.

bridgehead A forward position, seized by advancing troops in enemy territory, that serves as a base for more advances.

buffer zone A neutral area that lies between hostile forces and reduces the risk of conflict between them.

cease-fire During war, a temporary halt in fighting.

civil disobedience The deliberate breaking of the law by ordinary citizens, carried out as nonviolent protest.

civilian A person who is not a soldier.

coalition A temporary partnership of two or more groups or countries to achieve a particular goal.

conservative Wanting to preserve traditional ways of life, including institutions and standards of behavior.

curfew An official restriction on people's movements, requiring them to stay indoors for specified periods.

demilitarized zone An area where the opposing sides of a conflict are not allowed to station their forces.

division In an army, a self-contained military unit that is capable of sustained operations.

Druze Having to do with a religious sect that is similar to Islam and has followers mainly in Lebanon and Syria.

ethnic Having to do with a group of people of the same race, culture, religion, or place of origin.

exodus A departure from a place of a large number of people.

faction A group existing within a larger group that holds views not always in agreement with that larger group.

Holocaust The systematic extermination of nearly six million Jews by the Nazis during World War II.

Gaza Strip A narrow stretch of land in Palestine on the coast of the eastern Mediterranean Sea. It has been occupied by Israel since 1967, but partial control has been given to the Palestinian Authority since 1994.

Golan Heights A region overlooking Israel's upper Jordan River Valley. Israel took over the region in 1967 and annexed it from Syria in 1981, but the annexation is not recognized by Syria, the United States, or the UN.

guerrilla Having to do with a kind of warfare involving small, mobile groups of soldiers who are not part of a regular army and who often use hit-and-run ambush attacks to fight against more heavily armed forces.

intelligence Information about secret plans or activities, especially those of foreign governments.

Islamic Having to do with Islam, a religion established in the seventh century A.D. that is based on the teachings of an Arabian named Muhammad. According to Islam, Muhammad is the prophet of Allah, the one true God.

kibbutz A commune in Israel, especially one for farming. The plural of kibbutz is kibbutzim.

Knesset The legislative assembly of Israel.

legitimacy The quality of being legitimate, or conforming to recognized laws, rules, or standards.

lobby Attempt to persuade a government or influential person or group to support a particular cause.

mandate An official command or instruction from an authority, such as a government or organization.

Maronites Followers of a Christian sect based chiefly in Lebanon but also found in Palestine, Syria, Cyprus, and the United States.

mediator A person who works with both sides in a dispute in an attempt to help them reach an agreement.

Middle East A region located in southwest Asia and northwest Africa that includes the Arabian Peninsula and the countries of Egypt, Israel, Jordan, Saudi Arabia, Lebanon, Cyprus, Kuwait, Syria, Turkey, Iran, and Iraq as well as the occupied territories.

militant Intensely active in support of a cause, often to the point of conflict with other people or institutions.

militia A group of people who can arm themselves and carry out military operations for defense or for a cause but are not members of an official armed forces.

multilateral Involving more than two sides.

Muslims Followers of Islam.

nationalism Belief in the right of one's people to exist as a nation, or belief that one's nation is superior to others.

nationalize Transfer a business or industry from private to governmental control.

Nazi Party The National Socialist Party, which came to power in Germany under Adolf Hitler in 1933.

Occupied territories Regions taken over by Israel in 1967, including the West Bank and the Gaza Strip.

Ottoman Empire A Turkish empire that was established in the late thirteenth century in Asia Minor and eventually extended through the Middle East. The empire came to an end in 1922.

Palestinian Authority (PA) A Palestinian institution with limited powers of government over the Palestinians living in the West Bank and Gaza Strip.

Palestinian Liberation Organization (PLO) An organization that was founded in 1964 to represent Palestinian refugees in the Middle East but which is now an umbrella group representing various Palestinian factions seeking an independent Palestinian nation.

preemptive strike An attack carried out on an enemy before the enemy has had a chance to strike first.

reconnaissance The exploration of an area, especially to gather intelligence about enemy forces.

refugee A person who goes to another country to escape persecution, war, or natural disaster.

regime A system of government, or a group of people who rule a country.

resolution A proposal that has been voted upon by an official body, such as the UN.

secular Not involving religion or religious institutions.

settlement A newly established community.

Shi'ite A follower of the Shia branch of Islam, which considers Ali, a relative of Muhammad, and his descendants to be Muhammad's true successors.

sovereign territory A region legitimately controlled by a government.

Soviet Union A communist nation that was made up of Russia and neighboring republics and existed from 1922 to 1991.

strafe Attack an enemy on the ground with machine-gun or cannon fire from a low-flying aircraft.

terrorism The use of violence against civilians in order to achieve political aims.

tacit Understood or implied without being stated openly.

UN General Assembly The main debating body of the United Nations, composed of representatives of all member states.

United Nations An organization of nations formed in 1945 to promote peace, security, and international cooperation.

UN Security Council A body of UN member nations that is entrusted with maintaining international peace and security.

West Bank A region of Palestine located directly west of the Jordan River, between the river and Israel. It has been occupied by Israel since 1967, but since 1994 partial control has been given to the Palestinian Authority.

Zionism A worldwide movement that sought to establish a Jewish nation in Palestine. Since the founding of Israel in 1948, Zionists have continued to act in support of it.

STATISTICS

Casualty Levels

Approximate number of people killed in all the Arab-Israeli conflicts fought since 1948:

Israel	12,000
Egypt	24,000
Syria	8,500
Jordan	7,000
Palestinians	7,000 (since 1982)

Distribution of the Palestinian Population and Jewish Settlers in the West Bank and Gaza Strip Since 1967

Year	Palestinians (West Bank)	(Gaza)	Jews (West Bank/Gaza)
1967 (Dec 1)	604,494	380,800	–
1979	791,000	447,700	3,176 (1976)
1984	896,000	509,900	16,119 (1981)
1988	977,000	588,500	60,500 (1986)
1990	1,075,531	622,016	98,750 (1991)
1997	1,873,476	1,022,207	165,000
2002	1,932,637	1,087,067	226,028

Source: Jerusalem Fund for Education and Community Development; Israeli Central Bureau of Statistics; USAID West Bank and Gaza

Global Distribution of Palestinian People

Country	1986	1990–91	1995	2000
Jordan	1,398,050	1,824,179	2,170,101	2,596,986
West Bank/ East Jerusalem	951,530	1,075,531	1,227,545	1,383,415
Gaza	545,100	622,016	726,832	837,699
Israel	608,200	730,000	800,755	919,453
Lebanon	271,434	331,757	392,315	463,067
Syria	242,474	301,744	357,881	410,599
Remaining Arab Nations	582,894	445,195	516,724	599,389
Rest of World	280,846	450,000	500,000	550,000
Total	**4,880,518**	**5,780,422**	**6,692,153**	**7,760,608**

Source: Jerusalem Fund for Education and Community Development

Jewish Population Distribution in Palestine (1880–1947)

Year	Palestinians Numbers (%)	Jews Numbers (%)
1880	300,000 (94)	24,000 (6)
1917	504,000 (90)	56,000 (10)
1922	666,000 (89)	84,000 (11)3
1931	850,000 (83)	174,096 (17)
1936	916,061 (72)	384,078 (28)
1945/6	1,242,000 (69)	608,000 (31)
1947 (UN Partition)	1,300,000 (67)	640,298 (33)

Jewish Land Ownership in Palestine (1880–1947)

Year	Land ownership (cumulative) dunums*	% of land
1880	n/a	n/a
1917	650,000	less than 3
1922	751,192	3
1931	1,171,529	4
1936	1,380,578	5
1945/6	1,588,365	6
1947 (UN Partition)	1,900,000	7

* 1 dunum = 10,764 square feet (1,000 sq m)

Source: *Facts and Figures on Palestine* (Washington, D.C.: Palestine Center, 1991)

Distribution of Palestinian Refugees Registered with UN Relief and Works Agency (2003)

Region	No. of Camps	Registered Refugees	Registered Refugees in Camps
Jordan	10	1,718,767	304,430
Lebanon	12	391,679	225,125
Syria	10	409,662	119,766
Gaza Strip	8	907,221	478,854
West Bank	19	654,971	176,514
Total	**59**	**4,082,300**	**1,301,689**

Source: United Nations Relief and Works Agency for Palestine Refugees in the Near East, June 30, 2003

FURTHER INFORMATION

RECOMMENDED BOOKS

Bard, Mitchell, ed. *The Founding of the State of Israel.* Greenhaven Press, 2003.

Broyles, Matthew. *The Six-Day War* (*War and Conflict in the Middle East* series). Rosen Publishing, 2004.

Downing, David. *Yasser Arafat.* (*Leading Lives* series). Heinemann, 2002.

Harris, Nathaniel. *Israel and the Arab Nations in Conflict* (*New Perspectives* series). Raintree/Steck-Vaughn, 1999.

Rosaler, Maxine. *Hamas: Palestinian Terrorists* (*Inside the World's Most Infamous Terrorist Organizations* series). Rosen Publishing, 2003.

Ross, Stewart. *The Arab-Israeli Conflict* (*Witness to History* series). Heinemann, 2004.

RECOMMENDED VIDEOS

The 50 Years War: Israel and the Arabs (2000), PBS Home Video

Frontiers of Dreams and Fears (2003), Arab Film Distribution

Israel: Birth of a Nation (2001), A & E Home Video

Israel & Palestine (2003), Discovery Channel

RECOMMENDED WEB SITES

http://historyteacher.net/Arab-Israeli_Conflict.htm
A list of links to various web sites on Israel and the Palestinians.

www.merip.org/palestine-israel_primer/toc-pal-isr-primer.html
A concise history of the Arab-Israeli conflict from the Middle East Research and Information Project.

www.pbs.org/wgbh/pages/frontline/shows/oslo
This PBS web site looks at the Israeli-Palestinian conflict since the Oslo Accords.

Note to parents and teachers

Every effort has been made by the publishers to ensure that these web sites are suitable for children; that they are of the highest educational value; and that they contain no inappropriate or offensive material. The nature of the Internet, however, makes it impossible to guarantee that the contents of these sites will not be altered. We strongly advise that a responsible adult supervise Internet access.

IMPORTANT PLACES

Temple Mount/Haram Al-Sharif The Temple Mount (known to Muslims as Haram Al-Sharif) is a hill in the eastern part of Jerusalem's Old City and is the site of two ancient Jewish temples. Since the seventh century, it has also been a place of Muslim worship. It is the world's holiest site for Jews and the third holiest site for Muslims, and it also a place of special significance to Christians.

Dome of the Rock This famous Islamic mosque was built between 687 and 691 A.D. The rock in the center of the dome is believed by Muslims to be the spot to which Muhammad was brought by night and from which he ascended through the heavens to God.

Wailing (Western) Wall This outer courtyard wall is all that remains of the second Jerusalem Temple, the holiest building in Judaism, destroyed by the Romans about 2,000 years ago. It is a traditional site of prayer for Jews.

Al-Aqsa Mosque The Al-Aqsa Mosque is the largest mosque in Jerusalem and was completed in 710 A.D. It is believed to have been built on the site of the original Jerusalem Temple. The mosque has been the target of attacks by Jewish extremists.

ABOUT THE AUTHOR

The author, Alex Woolf, is an experienced writer and editor of children's information books, specializing in history and social issues at secondary level. His other books include *The World Wars: The Battle of Britain*, *Questioning History: Nazi Germany*, *Ideas of the Modern World: Fundamentalism*, *21st Century Debates: Terrorism*, and *World Issues: Genocide*.

INDEX